IDENTIFYING THE RIGHT PROJECT METRIC AND ITS IMPORTANCE

The Right Metric and Its Importance

You can only improve a process once you know exactly what you have to fix. Choosing the right metrics are the key levers that make the improvement quantifiable, making the practical problem a statistical statement and thus enabling a measurable improvement in the process.

Creating a quality drill down is extremely useful for identifying improvement opportunities for products, services and processes. However, many a time, many CTQs appear to be crucial to the improvement effort. It is important to select the right CTQ as a project metric, to avoid derailing the project execution.

I have witnessed innumerable situations where Black Belts have worked on non-critical metrics and later, have had to deal with unhappy customers. They worked on the wrong metric, which did not have the impact that the customer was expecting. Of course, there exist a number of books which have sections on project metrics; however, on the whole, very few specifics exist that offer focused guidance on how to select the right metrics.

This chapter attempts to explain with live examples and thus guide all practising quality professionals (Black Belts/Master Black Belts) in under-standing and selecting the right metrics for their improvement initiatives in the Lean and Six Sigma space.

This chapter includes the following sections:

- Why the right metric?
- What to keep in mind when choosing the right metric
- How to find the right metric
- Examples of successful projects, metrics, business cases and goal statements.

Why the right metric?

Defining the right metric impacts the process/project directly; this in turn has a direct impact on the end customer. It is one of the first steps you should take to develop a shared vision across the cross-functional project team. Getting it wrong here is like shooting aimlessly.

Some of the pitfalls of selecting the wrong metric:

➢ If the right metric is not selected, the customer may not fully comprehend the impact of the project, and the Black Belt's efforts will not be appreciated by internal/external stakeholders. For example, a project team for an accounts payable process wanted to improve the paid-on time percentage of the invoices billed; however, that would have negatively impacted the cash flow of the customer. The metric was refined to 'increase the paid on-time percentage for discounted vendors' to avoid discount loss.

➢ The Black Belt/Master Black Belt leading the project can face unnecessary challenges because:

- Poorly constructed metrics make it difficult to collect data and establish the right relation of project Y and potential Xs. For example, if productivity per day is the metric and X is agent tenure, it is very hard to relate the data of X with Y, as all the agents with different tenure work daily. However, taking a metric on reducing cycle time is a far better option for the agent's tenure, as shown in the table below:

Transaction No.	Cycle Time	Agent's Name	Tenure of Agent
12 abc1	22.6 minutes	Paul	3 months

Things to keep in mind while choosing the right metric:

➤ The metric should be selected on the smallest unit of the process, because if the smallest unit is set right, the entire process is bound to be right. Work on **direct metric** not on derived metric.

The rule to be followed here is that data on Y, once selected, should not be changed depending on the Xs, where Y is the smallest unit and is kept constant. It sets out the right relations with various Xs. However, if Y is not taken as the smallest unit, the values of Y will keep with each changing X, as you establish the X and Y relation.

Relation of Project Y with X

One of the important concepts of Six Sigma is to understand the relationship between Project Y and X, impacting the Y. If we refer to equation $Y=F(X)$, Y is a dependent variable and X is an independent variable. If we change X, Y will be impacted.

Pick up **the actual cause of a customer's problem as the project metric.** Customers will always give you a practical problem; convert it to a statistical statement.

E.g.: Practical problem: I am not happy with the process quality.
Statistical problem: To reduce the number of defects from 20% to 5% by April 2012.

➤ Avoid dollar value as a metric, like reducing the day's sales outstanding (DSO) $30 K per day to $25 K per day. Use business impact to highlight dollar values and impact. Always choose metrics like improving hit rates of calls from 25% to 45%, hence reducing DSO. In this example, the business impact could be a DSO reduction of $5 K per day.

> Some common metrics that can be selected are cycle time (variation reduction, mean shift), defect reduction, etc.

How to find the right metric

For every product or service, there could be multiple critical to quality characteristics. Focus on the CTQs that are most important to your customers. I recommend establishing the CTQ drill down tree, which helps to identify a relationship between the business Y and project Y. There are other tools available too, to identify whether the metric picked for the improvement project is the right metric. Let me illustrate this using regression analysis.

A major insurance company wanted the **dollar** value of renewed policies to go up; however, to avoid chasing dollar values as metrics, regression analysis was used to show a strong correlation between the number of policies renewed (count) vs. the value, thus securing the customer's approval for the metric on policies renewed (count) to be improved. See Figure 1.

CTQ Drill Down Tree

Amongst the various Six Sigma tools, Critical to Quality (CTQ) Trees is a tool that helps quality professionals to translate broad customer needs into specific, actionable, measurable project metrics. It also establishes a relationship between the Customer CTQ and Project CTQ. In other words, it helps to confirm to the Black Belts that the problem they are trying to solve through their Lean Six Sigma project is aligned to the customer/business priority and hence it will get the stakeholder's (customer/ sponsor's) approval on the business case of the project. Refer to the example of a CTQ drill down tree below.

Fitted Line Plot
Dollar Value = 8.93E+08 + 1093 Count of Policies

S	197981414
R-Sq	99.4%
R-Sq(adj)	99.3%

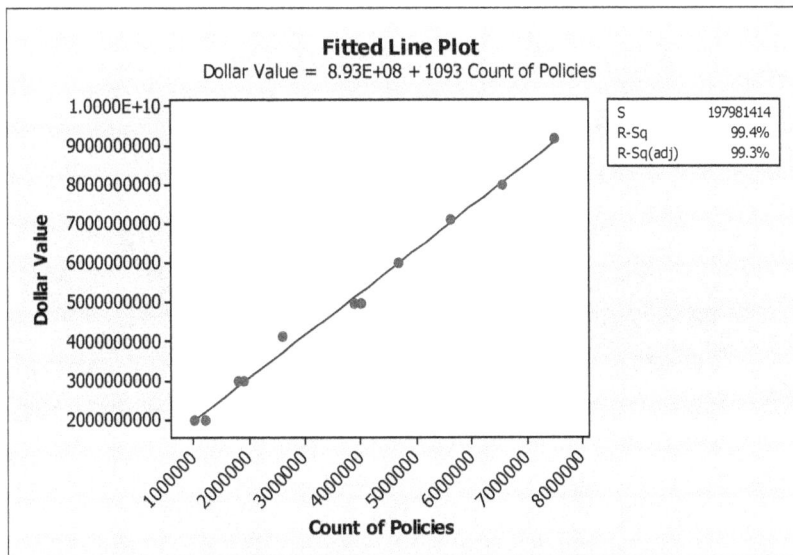

Figure 1 – Correlation of number of policies renewed and value of renewals

Make sure that all measurements are linked to bottom-line results.

The next two examples highlight different cases of the same example. Case I illustrates how not to proceed and Case II demonstrates how you should identify and consider metrics.

Example 1: XYZ Company, a global leader in business process management services, uses process to help its customers power intelligence across their enterprise to run smarter operations, make smarter decisions and use smarter technology. One of our clients had a pain point in collecting money from its customers on time and hence wanted us to increase the productivity of agents per day. Case I for this example shows what would happen if XYZ Company were to collect data based on exactly what the customer requested.

Case I

Goal Statement: To increase the average daily activations* from 29 to 40 for a quarter by Dec 30, 2012.

Analysis: In Case I, the metric is not on the smallest unit and is a derived metric. The graph attached in Case I shows that there are days when there are fewer than 40 activations to process. Therefore, the target is not achievable on a daily basis.

In situations like these, the Black Belt/Master Black Belts should help the customer understand the Lean Six Sigma way of selecting the smallest unit as a metric, demonstrating that the right metrics will impact the company's bottom-line, as in Case II.

* Activation

The first click received from a potential customer (when browsing for the product/ service on xyz AdWords) for the advertisement prepared for a given advertiser's campaign.

* Activation turnaround time
The time taken to activate the ad campaign from the day the sale was made (to the advertiser) to use the xyz AdWords' service.

[Activate Date – Sale Date]

Case II

*TAT – Turnaround time

Goal Statement: To reduce the overall turnaround time for activations from an average of four days to two days by Dec 30, 2012.

Analysis: Case II focuses on the smallest measurable unit, where cycle time per activation is to be improved. This will result in collecting the money faster for the account. It is a better metric for both the internal and external customers.

The customer was insisting on productivity improvement, focusing on increasing the amount of daily work completed. The Black Belt's responsibility is to achieve the customer's goal, but definitely not to follow the customer's instructions. The Black Belt should look at the problem in a different way, and that is the quality added. If you reduce the process time to process the activation, ultimately you are increasing productivity. Hence, activation cycle time is a right metric.

Example 2: In another project, XYZ Company's customer wanted to increase the average dollar value of sales per call.

Case I

Goal Statement: To increase the average sales from $60 to $90 by Dec 30, 2012.

Analysis: In **Case I**, the problem with the metric is that it is a dollar metric. The end result of driving this metric is not in the improvement team's control. Even if the team succeeds in implementing all the identified improvements and the end customer does not want to buy high-priced products, the project will not be able to achieve the end result. Also, further discussions with the customer revealed that the true goal was to increase the overall dollar value of sales with the same number of calls received.

Case II

Goal Statement: To reduce consultation failures from 70% to 20% by Dec 30, 2012.

Analysis: Case II uses a general percentage metric. Each call offers an opportunity to consult the end users with the choice of right product, which leads to increase in sale. The hypothesis is that if the consultation failure is reduced it will lead to increase in sales, thereby generating more revenue for the customer.

The customer wants you to increase average sales from $60 to $90, but be aware that even when doing all the right things, you may still not be able to increase sales, as the end-result is customer dependent. However, if you reduce the consultation failure rate, then you will automatically increase the dollar value of sales made, so Case II uses the right metric.

Some examples of successful projects, their metrics, business cases and goal statements are provided in Table 1 for quick reference.

Table 1 – Examples of using the right metric

Metric	Business Case/Challenge	Goal Statement
Time to process	ABC process requires staff to investigate payment exception items to determine whether to pay, transfer to cover, reverse or return the customer-initiated payment. XYZ is one of the processes where the touch time per invoice is high and there is a scope to reduce it.	To reduce XYZ process touch time per invoice from median 20 seconds to median 18.5 seconds by April 2012.
	A structured loans provider, which offers specialised financing in asset-based loans, was facing the following challenges: • The cycle time from deal bookings to dispute resolution (post-deal audit) was 59 days • Delay in audit leads to delays in business reporting • Bank regulation requires business reporting to happen within 30 days.	To reduce the structured loan post-deal booking cycle time from 59 days to 30 days.
	An equipment financier provides lease finance options to corporations for office equipment like copiers, printers, fax machines, etc. • Business conducts due diligence (underwriting process) on customers' creditworthiness before financing • This involves multiple authentication steps such as verification through LexisNexis, etc. • Touch time for a transaction in vendor underwriting was high, leading to lower productivity and high overall cycle time.	To reduce the time taken to close the activity from 41 minutes to 25 minutes by Jan 2012.

Revenue generation/ business generation	An Australian banking major was facing the challenge of a long cycle time for loan disbursal to customers. Initial observations showed that exception rate or transfer rate (for **Not in Good Order** (NIGO) cases), during credit decision and contract preparation, contributed majorly towards an increase in rework and cycle time. The average exception rate was at 30%, leading to: • Longer cycle times and customer dissatisfaction • Loss of revenue due to end customer declines • Lower productivity due to rework • Bankers spending time away from customer interfacing/revenue-generating opportunities.	To reduce the median exception rate for **Not in Good Order** (NIGO) cases from 30% to 5%, adding **Australian dollar** UD 47 million in the loan books.
Loss/defect reduction	A leading American retail bank's debit card fraud prevention process is designed to prevent frauds on debit cards: • On an average, the process handles 37,000 transactions every month • If an account is incorrectly blocked, it leads to potential revenue loss for the bank and dissatisfied customers. On the contrary, every good block will help the business to reduce potential fraud loss • Good block percentage is 31.6%.	To increase good block percentage from 31.6% to 35%, resulting in potential fraud loss reduction of approximately 2 **million per annum.**
	An equipment financier provides lease finance options to corporations for office equipment like copiers, printers, fax machines, etc. • The accuracy of new deal bookings was 94.2% (DPU) • Inaccurate deals needed to be	To reduce the error rate from 5.8% to 2% by May 2012.

	rebooked, leading to increased cycle time and customer dissatisfaction • Errors in financial fields can lead to potential financial loss for the business.	
Cost reduction	Seat utilisation (SU) is one of the major cost drivers that has a direct impact on the bottom-line of a company. ABC is operating at an average SU ranging from 1.30 to 1.36 for the last 3 years, presenting a huge scope for improvement. As per a benchmark study conducted by XYZ for Project Agile, every 0.1 (10 basis points) improvement in SU improves the bottom line by $1 MM.	To improve ABC company's median SU by 10% from 1.33 to 1.50 by July 2010 without impacting customers and operations.

To summarise, the following points can serve as signals that the metrics you're using may not be the best selections for your project:

- Metrics for which you cannot collect accurate or complete data.
- Metrics that are complex and difficult to explain to others.
- Metrics that complicate operations and create excessive overheads.
- Metrics that cause employees to act not in the best interests of the business but just to 'meet their numbers'.

The right metric is the starting point of the improvement journey. It helps projects meet their target goals and helps customers solve their pain areas. The above chapter attempts to help Black Belts select the right metrics and drive improvements in the right direction. Those executing projects can re-examine their metrics and make their projects more impactful for customers.

Amongst the various Six Sigma tools, Drill Down Tree is a tool that helps quality professionals to translate broad customer needs into specific, actionable, measurable project metrics. It also establishes a relationship between the Customer Priorities and Project CTQ. In other words, it helps to confirm to the BB's that the problem they are trying to solve through their Lean Six Sigma project is aligned to the customer/business priority and hence it will get the stakeholder's (customer/sponsor's) approval on the business case of the project. Let us take some examples to understand the concept better.

Case 1: The CEO of a company tells his direct reports that his biggest agenda for the year is cost reduction. There are different heads sitting in that meeting, i.e. HR, logistics, sales and quality. Now, the Head of the Infrastructure & Logistic function, to understand the drill down priority, will take the following approach:

Step 1:

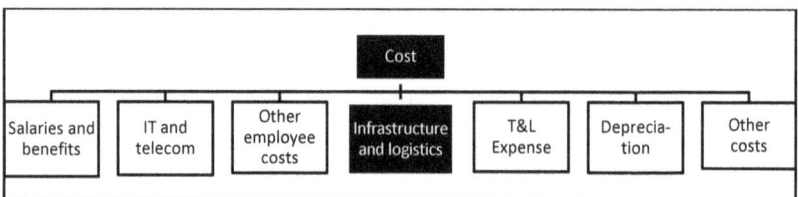

Their cost could be impacted through many different functions from salaries and benefits of the employees, IT and telecom, other employee costs, infrastructure and logistics, T&L expenses, to depreciation. However, for an infrastructure & logistics head, it is important to work on reducing the infrastructure and logistics cost only. The further drill down is as follows:

Step 2:

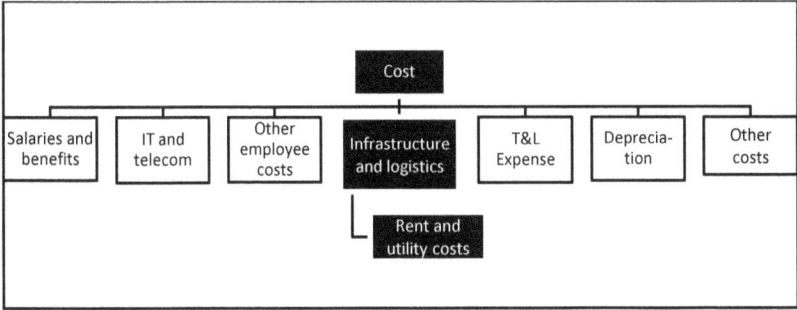

The next level of drill down of infrastructure & logistics will be 'rent & utility cost' for the organisation.

Step 3:

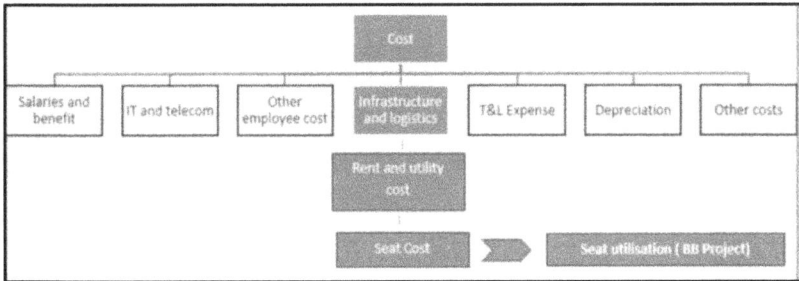

From the rent and utility cost, a further drill down will be the seat cost and the metric for the Black Belt's project could be improving seat utilisation from X% to Y%.

The drill down can stop here, as the project metric has been identified. A relationship has been established between Project Y and the Business Y.

Case 2: There is a leading American bank where the CEO has identified Profitability as the business priority and everyone in the business knows that the international wire transfer process is a big concern area in the organisation. Explained below is the drill down tree which will help relate Project Y with Business Y

Step 1:

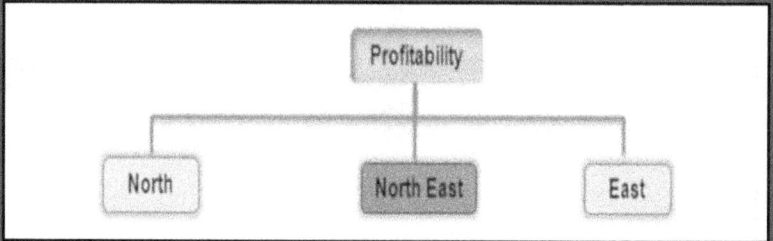

The Profitability of North, North East and East regions is evaluated; however, the North-East region shows minimum portability, hence it is identified as a level 2 drill down.

Step 2:

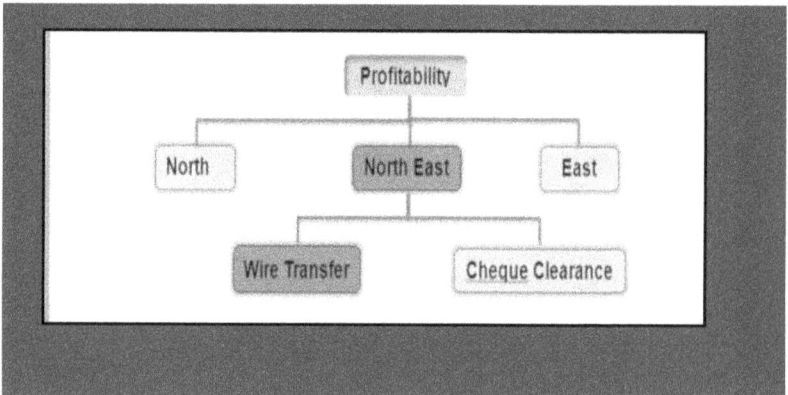

In North East region, there are two processes: wire transfer and cheque clearance, of which wire transfer is the low profitability process and hence is the process in focus for the BB project.

Step 3:

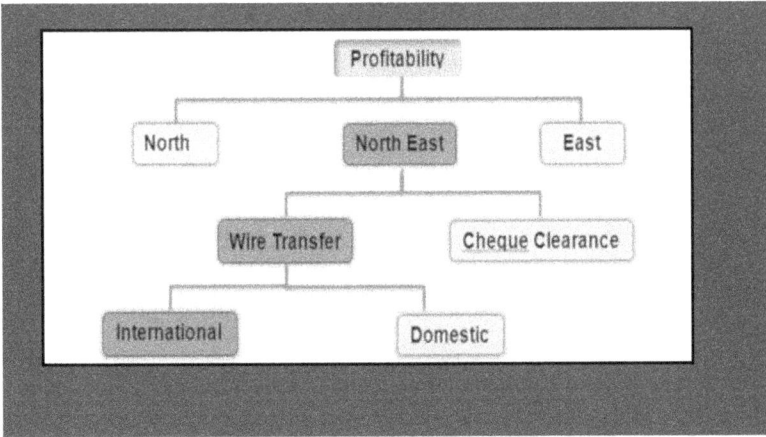

The main wire transfer process is further divided into two sub processes: international and domestic wire transfer. We have drilled down to international wire transfer as the problem we need to solve, therefore we do a project and identify the metric in the next step.

Step 4:

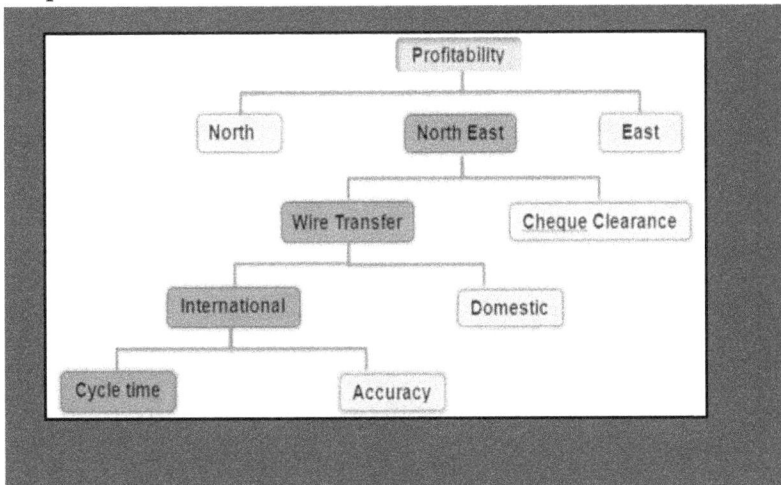

The Black Belt Project metric is identified as: 'To reduce the cycle time of international wire transfer from x minutes to y minutes by June 2013'. The drill down tree can now stop here as the project metric has been identified and we are able to establish a relationship between Project Y and Business Y.

Takeaway: Black Belts need to watch for the fact that there is no set rule to the level they can drill down. However, the thumb rule is as follows: go down to a maximum of five levels of drill down from the business priority.

DEFINE THE PROJECT

o   Back to Basics: Project Charter

What is a Project Charter?

A Project Charter is a tool to define the need of a project upfront. It is used to define the focus, scope, direction and motivation for a team. It has six elements:

1. Business Case
2. Problem Statement
3. Goal Statement
4. Project Scope
5. Project Team Charter
6. Milestones - Timeliness to finish the project.

Let us understand each of the elements in detail.

1. **Business Case:** Business Case presents the reason for a particular project. It is a citation written for any project to get management's approval. A good business case should answer three questions:

   I. What is the (brief) background of the business?
   II. Why should we do this project?
   III. What happens if the project is not done now?

   (1) *Business background: This is important if you are presenting your charter to someone very senior in the organisation who may not know in detail which part of the business will be impacted by your project. A brief background of the business is helpful in this scenario.*

      (a) *For example: ABC bank is a multinational, public sector banking and financial services company dealing with a number of offerings like home and car loans, insurance business and more.*

(2) **Why and what happens if the project is not done now:** *This is also important and needs to be explained to stakeholders...why this project is required and what is the loss to the organisation if this project is not done.*

(b) *For example: As a company, a bank's bad debt in loan books is exceeding the defined targets for the last two years. This is causing the bank cash flow problems and serious recovery strategy problems that is costing them $350 MN every year.*

Now club the two parts and get a perfect business case.

"ABC bank is a multinational, public sector banking and financial services company dealing with a number of offerings like home and car loans, insurance business and more. As a company, the bank's bad debt in loan books is exceeding the defined targets for the last two years. This is causing the bank serious cash flow problem that is costing them $350 MN every year."

(c) *Another example of a business case from a manufacturing company could be:*

"XYZ Company is a US-based earthmover company which deals with world-class earth movers and creates a variety of road rollers, bulldozer, crane, and graders. One of their department which deals with cranes is not meeting the final yield target of 97%. Overall, this is causing several rejections, and lower customer satisfaction that is costing the organisation $105 MN per annum and reduction in customer base by 5% every year."

2. **Problem Statement:** This explains the magnitude of the problem. In business case, there could be several issues highlighted; a single problem statement can help define the scope of the project.

A good problem statement should also include the information *on baseline data.*

(a) Let's continue with the examples dealt with in business case. Measured over the last six months, bad debt accounts in home loan books have increased by 15%, resulting in a loss of $85 MN.

(b) Measured over the last six months, the defective rate of products (cranes) from the factory has increased by 20%, resulting in a loss of $10.5 MN for six months cumulative.

3. **Goal Statement:** This defines the expected result from the project in defined timeliness. A Goal Statement should be SMART – Specific, Measurable, Attainable, Relevant and Timebound.

In the previous two examples, the goal statement will be:

(a) To reduce the bad debt accounts in home loan books from 25% to 10% by Dec 2016.

(b) To reduce the defective percentage in cranes from 10% to 3% by Oct 2016.

4. **Project Scope:** Scoping the project is important. Correct scoping can make or break the project.

Project Scope has two components: In Scope and Out of Scope.

Scope should also outline the specific details like geography, line of business and functional area.

Taking the previous two examples, the scope would be:

(a) **In Scope:** Bad debts account in the north, east and west regions for home loans only.

Out of Scope: All other bank products and southern region of home loans also.

(b) **In Scope:** Cranes made in Pinang - Malaysia

Out of Scope: Cranes made in other regions like Dallas in the US and Faridabad in India.

5. **Project Team Charter:** For the success of a project, it is important to define a correct team in the beginning. In a Six Sigma project, there are different roles defined.

   (1) **Sponsor:** Is responsible for keeping the project on track and towards a successful completion. The sponsor must fulfil several key duties related to the project. Like: launch of the project, signing off on milestones and sponsorship of monetary values if needed for the project. In a customer-driven project, a person with a designation like Sr. Vice President from the customer side could be a sponsor. (It is important to note that the sponsor should be able to approve cost, if needed, for that project).

   (2) **Champion:** Is responsible for the project. The champion is the owner of the project. The project is assigned by the sponsor to the champion and his role is to unite the project team and remove roadblocks. His other role is to give updates to the sponsor about the project at each phase and ensure honesty within the team.

   (3) **Mentor:** Is a Six Sigma certified resource like Master Black Belt or Black Belt that will help the team with the application of Lean Six Sigma methodologies and tools in the LSS Project.

   (4) **Team Members:** Are those who are part of the team and will help the project owner in data collection, brainstorming and then implementing solutions in the later stages of the project.

6. **Milestone:** This defines timeliness for different phases of the LSS project. Below is a template for the same.

   The thumb rule to define the timeliness is: assign two weeks to each phase apart from control. Allocate at least two months to control the improved situation.

	Start date	End date	Actual end date
Define			
Measure			
Analyse			
Improve			
Control			

What is the importance of the Project Charter?

A project charter is a snapshot of the project. It is an agreement between the management and the project team about what will be delivered though the project in the defined time and scope.

This is a document that formally authorises a project.

Note: In a project charter, 'business case' and 'problem statement' are for the 'management' to review and approve.

Goal statement, project scope, milestones and project team charter are for the 'project team'. The goal statement sets the expectation of what the team has to achieve, the scope within which they have to work, the milestones they have to meet, and their roles clearly defined so that each one of them can deliver as per the project's expectation.

A template of the project charter is given below.

Business Case	Scope

• Background of business
• Why should we do this project?
• What happens if this project is not done?
	• Outline specific details like
	  • Geography
	  • Line of Business
	  • Functional area

Problem Statement	**Milestones**
• Quantify the problem (if data is available) • Demonstrate the effect of problem	Start End • Define • Measure • Analyze • Improve • Control
Goal Statement	**Team Charter**
• S - Specific • M - Measurable • A - Attainable • R - Relevant • T - Time-bound	• Champion • Sponsor • Mentor • Process Owner • Team Members

○ COPIS/SIPOC

COPIS stands for Customer, Output, Process, Input and Supplier.

COPIS is a tool in tabular form that summarises the end-to-end business chain of one or more than one process, starting from the customer to suppliers.

COPIS can help give a high-level process view to those who are unfamiliar with the process, like people in higher management who have to give a go ahead to the project.

COPIS was earlier called SIPOC and it gave due importance to the voice of customers. It became a customer-centric tool which helped design the customised output.

This tool can help decide the scope of the project and, if worked out in detail, can provide clarity on the extent of the problem.

Let us understand it with the help of an example.

Find below the COPIS for a lipstick manufacturer.

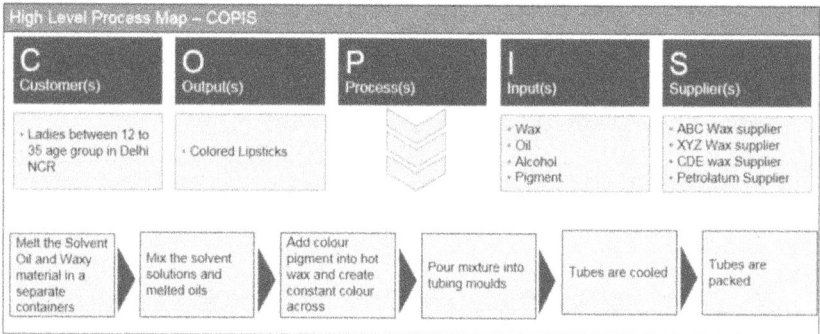

High Level Process Map – COPIS				
C Customer(s)	**O** Output(s)	**P** Process(s)	**I** Input(s)	**S** Supplier(s)
· Ladies between 12 to 35 age group in Delhi NCR	· Colored Lipsticks		· Wax · Oil · Alcohol · Pigment	· ABC Wax supplier · XYZ Wax supplier · CDE wax Supplier · Petrolatum Supplier
Melt the Solvent Oil and Waxy material in a separate containers	Mix the solvent solutions and melted oils	Add colour pigment into hot wax and create constant colour across	Pour mixture into tubing moulds	Tubes are cooled	Tubes are packed

The diagram above gives the E2E (end-to-end) process view to the high-level management, depicting the details of customer expectation, customised output designed, process followed, inputs procured and suppliers identified.

The COPIS tool can also help in identifying the cause of decline in sales. It helps to figure out which part of the E2E (end-to-end) chain is troubling.

Step 1 is to check the output of the E2E chain; if the quality of the lipsticks is not meeting customer requirements, then Step 2 would be used to evaluate the process.

During this evaluation, if it is found that the wax supplied by XYZ vendor is not good, action can be taken to caution the vendor to improve the quality of the input supplied or remove that particular vendor.

This is how COPIS can help us understand the E2E value chain and identify areas of improvement.

Hence this tool can not only give a high-level view but also could be an identifier for areas that require improvement.

○ Potential Impact

Before a project is taken to the management for approval, it is important to know the potential impact. Calculation of potential business impact provides the dollar value in terms of loss or gain to the business due to the project and hence, strengthens the business case. There are two types of impact: one is tangible and the other is non-tangible. Tangible impact is further divided into two types: the first is business impact and the second is P&L (profit and loss) impact. BI (business impact) impacts the top line of the business and P&L impacts the bottom line of the business.

There are different scenarios in a project which can lead to any one of these two types of tangible impacts.

- Increase in revenue and profits – BI and P&L
- Increase in revenue only – BI
- Increase in profits only – P&L
- Increase in cash flow and interest income – BI and P&L
- Loss reduction or cost avoidance leading to increase in profit – P&L.

Let us take some examples to understand these situations better.

Example 1: In a leading call centre, the outbound selling team is able to made 1500 successful calls (call where a sale is made) daily.

Base case: The average sale per call is $30; cost of operations (operating cost) is $15 per call; total revenue generated is 1500 x 30 = $45,000/-; total operating cost is 1500 x $15 = $22500/-; total profit = $45000 - $22500 = $22500.

BI Impact	Base Case	Case I	Case II	Case III
Successful calls	1500	2000	1500	1500
Average dollar sales per call	30	30	45	30
Operating cost	15	15	30	10
Total sales (Revenue)	45000	60000	67500	45000
Total Operating cost	22500	30000	45000	15000
P&L impact	22500	30000	22500	30000

Case 1: A productivity improvement project is done and successful calls per day have gone up to 2000 calls, keeping the operating cost the same. This would lead to increase in revenue by $15000, which means that the top line of the business has grown and overall profit has also gone up by $7500 ($30000 - $22500). This is impacting the bottom line of the business.

Case 2: The efficiency of the team has gone up and a sale per call has gone up by $15. In this case, the operating cost has also gone up by $15 per call. So, the total increase in revenue is $22500 ($67500 - $45000). This will impact the top line of the business. There is only one type of impact in this project.

Case 3: The operating cost per call has been reduced from base case by $5 ($15 - $10). Everything else remained the same but the overall profit of the business has gone up by $7500. There would only be one type of impact in this project.

Example 2: A project has been undertaken to reduce the DSO (daily sales outstanding – in how many days a company receives payment once the products are delivered) of a company. Before the project was initiated, the DSO was 80 days,

Cash Flow Impact	
Present DSO	80 days
Target DSO	75 days
Revenue Per day	$ 1,000,000
Cash flow	$ 5,000,000
Interest calculation Per day	$ 5,479.4
Annualized P&L impact	$ 2,000,000

which means the company received payment on the sold products after 80 days. The aim of the project was to reduce the DSO to 75 days. A sale made per day (revenue) is $1,000,000. Total cash flow impact of $5,000,000 means $5,000,000 is received five days early and this leads to an interest generation of $5479.4 {(Principal x Rate x Time /100) (5000000 x .08 x 5/365) rate of interest is 8% (0.08) and the time is 5 days divided by 365 days}. This is also impacting the bottom line of the business, so it is P&L impact.

Example 3: In the credit card dispute business, a bank has to do a chargeback to the customer within 120 days. If the bank misses the deadline, then it cannot chargeback customers and they have to write off the amount. This is a loss to the bank. A project was initiated to

Loss reduction		
Misses in Credit card dispute charge backs		
(count of cases/month)	1500	1000
Amount of chargeback per claim	$ 110	$ 110
Amount lost	$ 165,000	$ 110,000
Annualized Loss reduction		$ 660,000

reduce the misses in the count of chargeback cases (from 1500 to 1000). The amount of chargeback per case is $100 and the total loss reduction is $55,000 (1500 x $110 – 1000 x $110) per month. This is a P&L impact.

o   ARMI Chart & Communication Plan

ARMI Chart

The ARMI chart is a change management tool used to clearly identify the roles of each of the project team members during each phase of the project. This results in clarifying any ambiguity in the roles during the project.

ARMI stands for Approver, Resource, Member and Interested Party.

	Different Phases of Methodologies				
DMAIC	Define	Measure	Analyse	Improve	Control
8-Step Lean	Step 1	Step 3	Step 5	Step 7	Step 8
Project Sponsor	A	I	A	I	A
Project Champion	A	A	A	A	A
Six Sigma MBB	A	A	A	A	A
Business Leader	I	I	I	I	I
Black Belt	R	R	R	R	R
Subject Matter Expert	M	M	M	R	R
Trainer	M	M	M	R	M

A represents the approver; stakeholders who need to approve a particular phase of the project.

I represent the interested party; the stakeholder does not have to approve in that phase; however, they are only interested in the output delivered during that phase of the project.

R is the resource whose niche skills are required during the project; for example, Black Belt is a resource as he brings in Six Sigma tools and methodology skills. Somebody from IT whose help is needed to develop a macro in the improvement phase will become a resource during that phase.

M represents member of a project who is a part of the project and can help in various project-related activities like brainstorming, data collection, value-stream mapping, solution identification, etc...

Communication Plan

It is important to communicate the work done to the stakeholders at different stages of any project, hence a communication plan should be made and circulated at the beginning of the project.

The effectiveness of the communication plan will be evident once it is executed, so it needs to be implemented. A plan that is only on paper is no plan. Below is a template that can be used to formulate a communication plan.

Event	Message	Audience	Frequency	Responsibility	Medium
Project team meeting	Project progress update	Project team	Once/weekly	Project owner	Face-to-face meeting
Stakeholder review	Project update	Important Stakeholders	End of each phase	Project owner	Conference call
Project update	Progress made & next steps	All stakeholders	Bi-weekly	Project owner	Email

Case Study

In 2014, ABC Bank started losing business to their competitors and their customer base started shrinking, especially in the international wire transfer business.

The aim of the organisation is to increase their growth and customer satisfaction by increasing the speed of their service. ABC bank operates in four different regions (north, east, west & northeast)

The organisation has formed a cross-functional team to work on the opportunity identified, in which the goal is to reduce the cycle time of the international wire transfer process of the northeast region from four days to one day in the next three months. The growth expected from this project is $100MN of wire transfer increase in the next nine months and will give $10MN of P&L impact as service charges.

Data

Wire transfer No	Cycle time	City	Documented process available	Agent	Branch	Tenure	Shift	Day of week	Week of month	Cycle time after the improvements
1001	5.75	Del	N	1	CP	625	M	Mon	3	0.553919746
1002	4.61	Del	Y	2	CP	702	M	Tues	4	1.224144774
1003	2.96	Hyd	Y	3	JP	887	M	Thur	5	0.88237431
1004	4.65	Del	N	1	CP	694	M	Tues	3	0.691270916
1005	3.13	Hyd	Y	1	JP	867	M	Wed	1	1.105562947
1006	3.18	Hyd	Y	1	JP	848	M	Wed	2	1.384580225
1007	4.58	Del	N	2	CP	711	M	Tues	4	1.256025375
1008	3.50	Hyd	Y	2	JP	823	M	Wed	1	0.823771343
1009	4.01	Del	N	2	CP	762	M	Tues	5	1.079859032
1010	3.77	Hyd	N	2	CP	797	M	Wed	2	0.914839236
1011	4.03	Del	N	1	CP	754	M	Tues	3	0.781780614
1012	3.36	Hyd	Y	1	JP	831	M	Wed	1	1.147593726
1013	3.86	Hyd	N	1	CP	780	A	Wed	2	1.426768513
1014	4.05	Del	N	3	CP	745	A	Tues	4	0.971275672
1015	4.98	Del	N	3	CP	651	A	Tues	5	0.906386905
1016	4.07	Del	N	3	CP	737	A	Tues	3	1.181195678
1017	2.38	Hyd	Y	3	JP	890	A	Thur	4	1.035047309
1018	4.72	Del	N	3	CP	685	A	Tues	5	1.14493037
1019	3.97	Hyd	N	1	CP	771	A	Thur	3	0.815528876
1020	4.11	Del	N	1	CP	728	A	Tues	4	1.259155052
1021	6.12	Del	N	1	CP	616	A	Mon	5	0.36657666
1022	3.86	Hyd	N	1	CP	788	A	Wed	1	1.296985854
1023	3.02	Hyd	Y	1	JP	870	E	Wed	2	1.391925252
1024	4.81	Del	N	3	CP	659	E	Tues	3	1.332274366
1025	5.17	Del	N	3	CP	642	E	Mon	4	0.573195951
1026	4.75	Del	N	3	CP	676	E	Fri	1	1.29763058
1027	3.75	Hyd	N	3	JP	805	E	Wed	2	1.026905057
1028	3.33	Hyd	Y	1	JP	840	E	Wed	1	0.830184963
1029	4.79	Del	N	1	CP	668	E	Tues	5	0.807849465
1030	1.82	Hyd	Y	1	JP	900	E	Fri	2	1.03257614
1031	4.13	Del	N	1	CP	719	E	Tues	3	0.872637044
1032	3.16	Hyd	Y	2	JP	857	E	Wed	1	1.035014727
1033	6.58	Del	N	2	CP	608	E	Mon	4	0.947485172
1034	3.54	Hyd	N	2	JP	814	E	Wed	2	1.274075699
1035	5.21	Del	N	2	CP	633	E	Mon	5	1.417853328

REFER TO THE CASE STUDY AND PREPARE THE ABOVE-MENTIONED STEPS

Project Charter

Business Case:	Scope:
ABC Bank is a multinational bank dealing in several offerings like mortgages, home loans and money transfer. The bank is facing a challenge in retaining its customer base in its internal wire transfer business. This is due to a longer cycle time as compared to competitors. This is leading to a decline in business revenue. If this issue is addressed, the expected revenue growth is $100MN in the next nine months and it would lead to $10MN of P&L impact.	In scope: International wire transfer business in the North-East region. Out of scope - North, West and East & other businesses of the North-East region
Problem Statement:	**Milestone:**
Over the last nine months, ABC bank has been taking huge cycle time to process internal wire transfers and is losing this business rapidly to their competitors. This has led to huge loss of revenue and profitability.	Start End Define - 15th March, 2016 1 Week Measure - 22nd March, 2016 2 Weeks Analyse - 5th April, 2016 2 Weeks Improve - 19th April, 2016 5 Weeks Control - 10th June, 2016 5 Weeks
Goal Statement:	**Team Charter:**
To reduce the cycle time of international wire transfers in the North-East region from four days to one day by July 2016	Sponsor - VP of ABC Bank Champion – Regional Head Mentor - Master Black Belt - Lean Six Sigma Process Owner - Business Head of North-East region Team Members- Members from cross-functional team

High-level process map COPIS

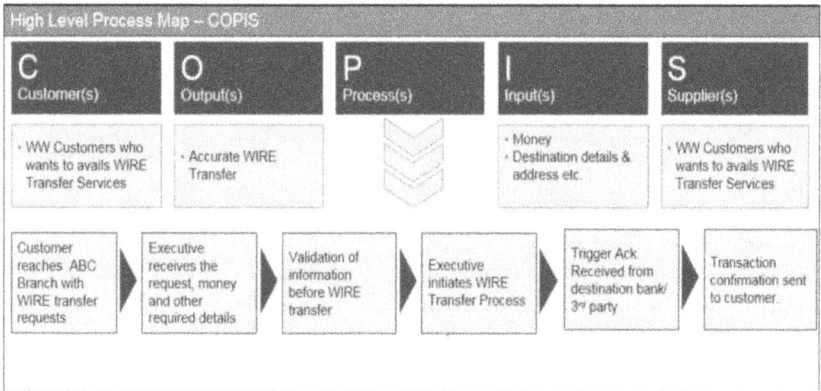

High Level Process Map – COPIS

C Customer(s)	O Output(s)	P Process(s)	I Input(s)	S Supplier(s)
· WW Customers who wants to avails WIRE Transfer Services	· Accurate WIRE Transfer		· Money · Destination details & address etc.	· WW Customers who wants to avails WIRE Transfer Services

| Customer reaches ABC Branch with WIRE transfer requests | Executive receives the request, money and other required details | Validation of information before WIRE transfer | Executive initiates WIRE Transfer Process | Trigger Ack Received from destination bank/ 3rd party | Transaction confirmation sent to customer. |

ARMI Chart and Communication Plan

Stakeholder	Define	Measure	Analyse	Improve	Control
Sponsor – VP, ABC Bank	A	I	A	A	A
Champion – Regional head, ABC Bank	A	A	A	A	A
Mentor	A	A	A	A	A
Process Owner - Business head	A	I	I	A	A
IT project manager	R	R	R	R	R
SME – Sr. wire transfer executive	M	M	M	M	M

Event	Message	Audience	Frequency	Responsibility	Medium
Stakeholder review	Discuss the project performance and plan ahead	Champion, sponsor & other business stakeholders	Monthly	Champion	One-on-one meeting
Six Sigma review	Review Six Sigma methodology and tools	Champion, sponsor, MBB and team members	As per the defined schedule	Six Sigma project lead	Meeting room
Project update	Progress made so far and next steps	Entire team and stakeholders	Fortnightly	Six Sigma project lead	Email

A – Approver, R – Resource, M – Member, I – Informed

Questions for 'Define' phase of DMAIC methodology.

Q1. What are the six elements of a project charter? What is the importance of each one of them?

Q2. What does ARMI stand for? What is the significance of this tool?

Q3. What is COPIS? Explain its importance.

○ Identifying Potential Xs

$Y=f(x)$ is a mathematical statement and it is used to explain that the project output (goal)(Y) is a result of the drivers (Xs) within the processes. The aim of the Six Sigma project is to find out which of the few input and process variables are impacting the project goal, Y. To do that, project leads can conduct a brainstorming activity and can use tools like fishbone diagrams to represent it.

There are basic thumb rules to conduct a brainstorming session to identify potential Xs. The rule is that one should have five to eight people in the room and in those five to eight people, one or two people should be from outside the core project team in order to give an outside-in perspective.

Fishbone

The fishbone diagram identifies many possible causes for an effect or problem (Project Y). It can be used to structure a brainstorming session. It immediately sorts ideas into useful categories.

The three different types of brainstorming techniques are:

• Chit Method: Participants write down their ideas on a piece of paper and hand it over to the person conducting the brainstorming.
• Random Technique: Each participant can speak at any time in the group meeting and the brainstorming lead writes down the ideas on the board.
• Round Robin Method: Each participant is given an opportunity to give an idea and that idea is noted on the C&F board.

Brainstorm the major categories of causes of the problem. If this is difficult, use generic headings:

Methods, Machines (equipment), People (manpower), Materials, Measurement & Environment.

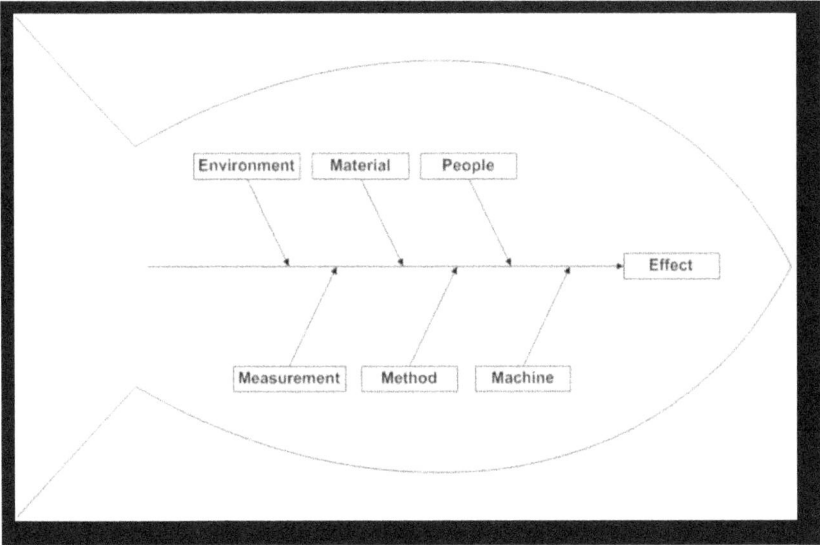

In service industries, it could be People, Process, Procedure, Place and Environment.

Once Potential Xs are identified, then they are categorised under two heads: process door Xs and data door Xs.

- **Process door:** These are Xs where data capturing is not possible. They are tackled via process door techniques like Nominal Group Technique, or other prioritisation techniques could be used to identify significantly impacting Xs.

- **Data door:** These are Xs where data is available or could be captured. To find out a significant X, hypothesis testing is used.

o Data Collection Plan

Data Collection – Plan & Template:

Collecting data in a DMAIC project is an important step; during reviews, I have seen lot of Black Belts make mistakes in collecting data and this impacts the overall improvement of the project/process.

A BB must adhere to the following eight steps to create a comprehensive plan.

Step 1: Identify whether Project Y is Continuous or Discrete.

Step 2: Write down the operational definition of Project Y. This is important as everyone involved in the team should understand Project Y in the same way. For example, a project on reducing the cycle time of a transaction can have different interpretations by different users if an operational definition of the cycle time is not there.

The operational definition must have the mathematical formula, if required, to be used.

Step 3: Identify unit, defect, opportunities and specification limits for Project Y; it is important to establish the above mentioned before you proceed to a data collection plan.

Step 4: Identify potential Xs for Project Y; it is also very important to collect data on Xs along with Y in one go.

Step 5: Write down the operational definitions for Xs as well.

Measure Name	Cycle time for each wire	Branch	Associate	Break time	Shift
Measure Type (Y or X)	Y	X1	X2	X3	X4
Data Type (continuous/ discrete)	Continuous	Discrete	Discrete	Continuous	Discrete
Operational Definition	Time taken to process a wire Start point: when account no is keyed into the system End point: when account is closed in the system	Office in which the wire transfer is initiated	Officer who is processing the wire	Any break taken by the associate is considered. It could be a break from work for query resolution or tea/coffee	Shift in which the associate received the request (morning/ evening)

Step 6: Now identify a statistically validated sample through Minitab or any other tool. Remember, the sample picked must represent the characteristics of the population. BBs can use different sampling techniques to identify a sample.

Step 7: Create a data collection plan: 4W1H is a simple LSS tool which can be used to create the data collection plan

Four W: what, when, where, who

One H: how

For example:

Measure Name	Wire Transfer Cycle Time	Branch	Associate	Break time	Shift
What is to be done	Capture data on cycle time	Capture data on branch	Capture data on associate	Capture break time data	Capture data on shift
When it is to be done	Daily	Daily	Daily	Daily	Daily
Where it is to be done	Data Collection Template	Data Collection Template	Data Collection Template	Data Collection Template	Data Collection Template
How it is to be done	Extract international wire transfer report and exclude scope requests	Extract international wire transfer report where branch ID is captured	Extract international wire transfer report in which agent ID is captured	Extract time on system report to capture break time per associate	Record the time of processing that wire, which can give us the shift data
Who will do it	Member 1	Member 1	Member 1	Member 2	Member 2

Step 8: Once the data collection plan is ready, now create a data collection template in which the data will be captured.

Wire No.	Account No.	Branch	Associate	Break time (mins)	Shift

How to capture data for uniformity:
1. Capture the unique wire transfer number in column one.
2. Capture the account number and relevant details of the same wire adjacent to 'wire number' in the same column.

Wire No.	Account No.	Branch	Associate	Break time (mins)	Shift
123A123	ASQ12345	ABC	Agent 1	50	Morning

3. Repeat the same process for the rest of the wires picked in the random sample.

Wire No.	Account No.	Branch	Associate	Break time (mins)	Shift
123A123	ASQ12345	ABC	Agent 1	50	Morning
345B567	ASQ12346	XYZ	Agent2	45	Evening

If BBs create the data collection plan in the above-mentioned way and capture data as suggested, then the 'analyse' phase and the remaining improvements will be highly effective.

○ Gage R&R

In any process, there are two types of variation that exist: one is measurement system variation and the second is process variation. LSS projects are done to reduce the process variation; however, sometimes, there are measurement system variations present that are more than the permissible limit and are unknown, which can be very lethal for the success of a project.

One of the tools to identify the measurement system variation is **Attribute Gage R&R**, where R&R stands for repeatability and reproducibility.

Attribute Gage checks three things:
1. Repeatability: within the individuals
2. Reproducibility: between the individuals
3. Accuracy: that all the results are matching the standard.

To pass Gage, 'all appraisals Vs standard' should be greater than 90%.

How to conduct Attribute Gage R&R

Consider a business where transactions are processed or it's a call centre business:

Step 1: Take a minimum of 20 unique transactions or 20 unique calls. Ask the quality checkers of the calls or transactions to monitor them and give their score on the calls/transactions as defective or non-defective.

Step 2: Ask a customer/subject matter expert to monitor the same transactions. This will be used as a standard to check the accuracy of the QC (quality checker) resources.

Step 3: After two weeks, ask the QC resources to monitor the same transactions/calls and score them again as defective/non-defective. This is to check repeatability of the resources.

A minimum of two resources and two trials for Attribute Gage R&R are a must.

Attribute Gage R&R can be performed in Excel. For example, Gage is done for two QC resources and there are two trials. Twenty-five unique transactions are taken and the outputs are stored as follows:

Transaction No.	Trial 1			Trial 2		Gage Result
	QC 1	QC 2	Standard	QC1	QC2	All Appraisers Vs Standard
1	Non-Defective	Non-Defective	Non-Defective	Non-Defective	Non-Defective	Pass
2	Defective	Defective	Defective	Defective	Defective	Pass
3	Non-Defective	Non-Defective	Non-Defective	Non-Defective	Non-Defective	Pass
4	Defective	Defective	Defective	Defective	Defective	Pass
5	Non-Defective	Non-Defective	Non-Defective	Non-Defective	Non-Defective	Pass
6	Non-Defective	Non-Defective	Non-Defective	Non-Defective	Non-Defective	Pass
7	Non-Defective	Defective	Non-Defective	Non-Defective	Defective	Fail
8	Defective	Defective	Defective	Defective	Defective	Pass
9	Non-Defective	Non-Defective	Non-Defective	Non-Defective	Non-Defective	Pass
10	Non-Defective	Non-Defective	Non-Defective	Non-Defective	Non-Defective	Pass
11	Non-Defective	Non-Defective	Non-Defective	Non-Defective	Non-Defective	Pass
12	Defective	Defective	Defective	Defective	Defective	Pass
13	Non-Defective	Non-Defective	Non-Defective	Non-Defective	Non-Defective	Pass
14	Non-Defective	Non-Defective	Non-Defective	Non-Defective	Non-Defective	Pass
15	Defective	Defective	Defective	Defective	Defective	Pass

16	Non-Defective	Non-Defective	Non-Defective	Non-Defective	Non-Defective	Pass
17	Defective	Non-Defective	Defective	Defective	Non-Defective	Fail
18	Non-Defective	Non-Defective	Non-Defective	Non-Defective	Non-Defective	Pass
19	Non-Defective	Non-Defective	Non-Defective	Non-Defective	Non-Defective	Pass
20	Defective	Defective	Defective	Defective	Defective	Pass
21	Non-Defective	Defective	Non-Defective	Defective	Non-Defective	Fail
22	Defective	Defective	Defective	Defective	Defective	Pass
23	Non-Defective	Defective	Non-Defective	Non-Defective	Non-Defective	Fail
24	Non-Defective	Non-Defective	Non-Defective	Defective	Non-Defective	Fail
25	Non-Defective	Defective	Defective	Non-Defective	Defective	Fail

Interpretation

All the rows which have the same values, like defectives/non-defectives in all the columns, will be pass. To explain this concept further, let's understand transactions 1 and 25 in detail.

For transaction 1, all the resources and standard values were non-defective and hence repeatability, reproducibility and accuracy are fine, hence this is pass.

For transaction 25, QC 1 is saying it is a non-defective transaction in both the trials but standard is saying it is a defective transaction, hence QC 1 has accuracy issues and the overall Gage fails.

So overall, Gage percentage is calculated based on the 'total pass/total transactions gaged' and that is 19/25 (76%). This means attribute gage failed.

Next steps if Gage fails:

First find out where the issues are and then make improvement plans and execute them. Check gage again after improvements; only if it passes should you proceed to data collection in your project.

Issue identification for improvement plan

1. Repeatability issue: For transaction 23, QC2 said in the first trial that it is defective but in the second trail said it is non-defective, hence it is not able to repeat itself and hence there's an issue.
2. Reproducibility issue: In transaction 25, QC1 said non-defective and QC2 said defective, which means they both have different outputs for the same type of work, meaning they are not reproducible.
3. Accuracy: Wherever the response of QC1 and QC2 are not matching with the standard there is an accuracy issue.

When you create an improvement plan, you need to keep in mind that the plan for QC1 can be different from QC2.

How to perform attribute Gage R&R in Minitab

Step 1: Paste data as shown below.

	C1	C2-T	C3-T	C4-T	C5-T	C6-T	C7
	Transaction no	QC 1	QC 2	Standard	QC1	QC2	
1	1	Non-Defective	Non-Defective	Non-Defective	Non-Defective	Non-Defective	
2	2	Defective	Defective	Defective	Defective	Defective	
3	3	Non-Defective	Non-Defective	Non-Defective	Non-Defective	Non-Defective	
4	4	Defective	Defective	Defective	Defective	Defective	
5	5	Non-Defective	Non-Defective	Non-Defective	Non-Defective	Non-Defective	
6	6	Non-Defective	Non-Defective	Non-Defective	Non-Defective	Non-Defective	
7	7	Non-Defective	Defective	Non-Defective	Non-Defective	Defective	
8	8	Defective	Defective	Defective	Defective	Defective	
9	9	Non-Defective	Non-Defective	Non-Defective	Non-Defective	Non-Defective	
10	10	Non-Defective	Non-Defective	Non-Defective	Non-Defective	Non-Defective	
11	11	Non-Defective	Non-Defective	Non-Defective	Non-Defective	Non-Defective	
12	12	Defective	Defective	Defective	Defective	Defective	
13	13	Non-Defective	Non-Defective	Non-Defective	Non-Defective	Non-Defective	
14	14	Non-Defective	Non-Defective	Non-Defective	Non-Defective	Non-Defective	
15	15	Defective	Defective	Defective	Defective	Defective	
16	16	Non-Defective	Non-Defective	Non-Defective	Non-Defective	Non-Defective	
17	17	Defective	Non-Defective	Defective	Defective	Non-Defective	
18	18	Non-Defective	Non-Defective	Non-Defective	Non-Defective	Non-Defective	
19	19	Non-Defective	Non-Defective	Non-Defective	Non-Defective	Non-Defective	
20	20	Defective	Defective	Defective	Defective	Defective	
21	21	Non-Defective	Defective	Non-Defective	Defective	Non-Defective	
22	22	Defective	Defective	Defective	Defective	Defective	
23	23	Non-Defective	Defective	Non-Defective	Non-Defective	Non-Defective	
24	24	Non-Defective	Non-Defective	Non-Defective	Defective	Non-Defective	
25	25	Non-Defective	Defective	Defective	Non-Defective	Defective	

Current Worksheet: Worksheet 1

Step 2 : Follow the path in Minitab - 'Stat>Quality tool>Attribute agreement analysis'.

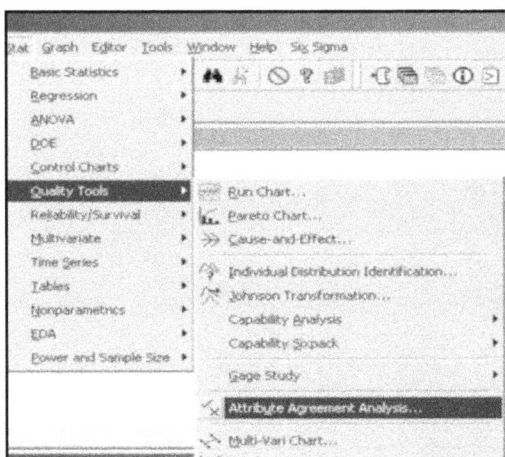

Step 3: Select multiple columns and then select both trials of QC1 together and select both trials for QC2 together.

1. Enter 2 in No. of appraisers, as we are doing gage for two appraisers
2. Enter 2 in number of trials, as we have taken two trials
3. Enter the name of QC resources. This is optional
4. Enter standard data column in known standard/attribute. This is also optional.

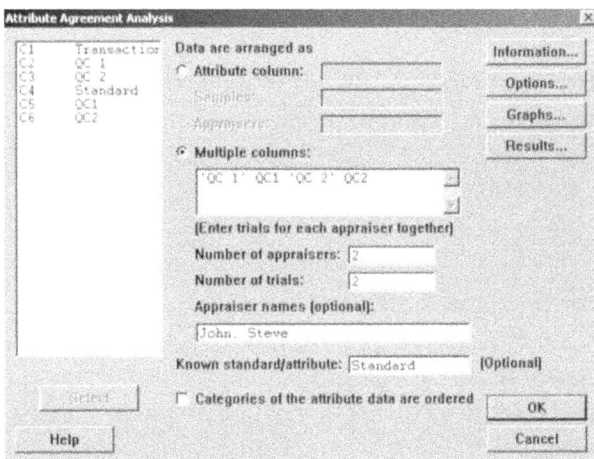

Step 4. Take out data from the screen and arrange it in the below-defined format.

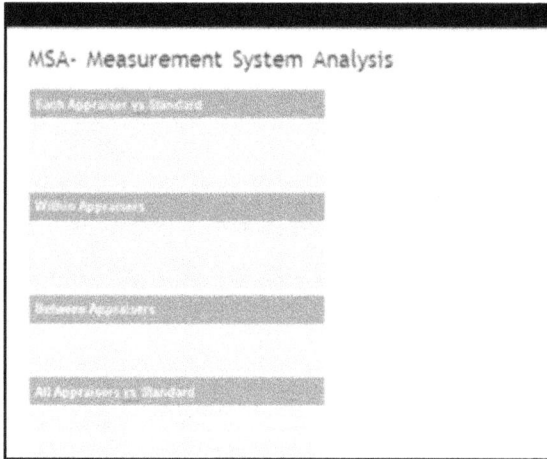

And the data will look like:

1. Overall Gage

All Appraisers vs Standard

Assessment Agreement

Inspected Matched Percent 95% CI
25   19 (76.00) (54.87, 90.64)

Total inspected transactions 25 and matched 19, overall gage (19/25) is 76%

2. Repeatability

Within Appraisers

Assessment Agreement

Appraiser Inspected Matched Percent 95% CI
John 25   23 (92.00) (73.97, 99.02)
Steve 25   23 (92.00) (73.97, 99.02)

Repeatability of both the resources is at 92%, which means they both pass the repeatability test.

3. Reproducibility
Between Appraisers

Inspected Matched Percent 95% CI
 25   19 76.00 (54.87, 90.64)

Reproducibility of both the resources is at 76%, which means they both fail the reproducibility test.

4. Accuracy
Each Appraiser vs Standard

Assessment Agreement

Appraiser Inspected Matched Percent 95% CI
John,   25   22   88.00   (68.78, 97.45)
Steve   25   21   84.00   (63.92, 95.46)

Accuracy at the individual level is a problem as both are not meeting the standard - three times for John and four times for Steve.

Once you have identified the overall gage issues, create individual improvement plans and proceed.

Once the Gage R&R is passed, one can go ahead and collect data and start the analysis.

REFER TO CASE STUDY AND CREATE THE ABOVE STEPS

Identify Potential Xs through brainstorming (fishbone) with the team.

Data collection plan

Measure Name	Cycle time	City	Process documen-tation	Agent	Tenure	Shift	Day of the week	Week of the month	Branch
Measure Type (Y/X)	Y	X	X	X	X	X	X	X	X
Data Type (Cont or Disc)	Continuous	Discrete	Discrete	Discrete	Continuous	Discrete	Discrete	Discrete	Discrete
Operational Definition	Person gets a token to meet representative till amount is wired	Place for which the wire is initiated	Determines whether documents are available for each process	Person processing wire transfer; should be trained and tested on the process	No. of total days since agent has been working in the wire transfer process	Wire transfer happened during day or evening shift	(Mon to Fri) when the wire transfer request is initiated	Which week of the month the wire is processed	The branch in which the wire is initiated
Who will collect	Team Member 1	Team Member 1	Team Member 1	Team Member 2	Team Member 1	Team Member 1	Team Member 1	Team Member 1	Team Member 2
By when	25 March 16	28 March 16	28 March 16	28 March 16	28 March 16	28 March 16	28 March 16	28 March 16	28 March 16

Questions for Measure phase

Q1. What are the different heads (causes) of a fishbone? What is the other name for fishbone?

Q2. What is the importance of a data collection plan, and how is it to be done?

Q3. What is Gage R&R? What is repeatability and reproducibility?

○ Identifying Process Stability & Normality (Run Chart & Normality)

Before we start analysing the data, we must check whether the sample data collected has no special causes. The tool that is used to identify special causes is Run Chart in Minitab.

Run Chart/Data Stability

It is important to do continuous improvement projects using data which doesn't have any special causes, as data with special causes can lead to incorrect interpretations (root causing) in the analyse and improve phase of a continuous improvement (Lean Six Sigma) project. There are many ways to identify special causes in a data set. As a Six Sigma practitioner and a Master Coach, I recommend the use of run charts to identify special causes and check for data stability.

Definition: Run Chart is a tool which will help identify the special causes. Run Chart plots all the individual observations versus the subgroup number, and draws a horizontal reference line at the median. When the subgroup size is greater than one, Run Chart also plots the subgroup means or medians and connects them with a line.

The two tests for non-random behaviour detect trends, oscillations, mixtures and clustering in your data. Such patterns suggest that the variation observed is due to special causes - causes arising from outside the system that can be corrected. Common cause variation is variation that is inherent or a natural part of the process. A process is in control when only the common causes affect the process output.

Importance: It is important to work on a data free from special causes. For example, you are doing a project to increase the productivity of the team and the data picked for the analysis is when you had fewer volumes (due to a special cause). Average transactions handled by the associates during less volume time are 30 but there is capacity to process 15 more documents per person. With this data as a baseline, Black Belt had initiated a project to increase productivity per associate from 30 to 40 transactions. Next month, the team started getting volumes as per capacity and associates performed at 45 transactions on their own; Black Belt, without initiating real improvements, will get the benefit of a project. Hence baseline data with special causes should be avoided.

In the other situation, where there is a special cause and volumes have increased, the team is already stretched in meeting the daily volumes and Black Belt has taken on a further target to improve productivity where the goal is to increase productivity from 45 to 55. In this kind of a situation, where the team is already overstretched, Black Belt will not be able to meet the target of the project initiated or it would be close to impossible. Hence it is important to select data which should have no special causes.

How to Create a Run Chart in Minitab

Step 1: Suppose there is a project on cycle time reduction, Step 1 is to check the stability of data. For that, paste the data of cycle time in C1. See the attachment below:

	C1	C2	C3	C4	C5	C6	C7
	Cycle time						
1	5.75						
2	4.61						
3	2.96						
4	4.65						
5	3.13						
6	3.18						
7	4.58						
8	3.50						
9	4.01						
10	3.77						
11	4.03						
12	3.36						
13	3.86						
14	4.05						
15	4.98						
16	4.07						
17	2.38						
18	4.72						
19	3.97						

Step 2

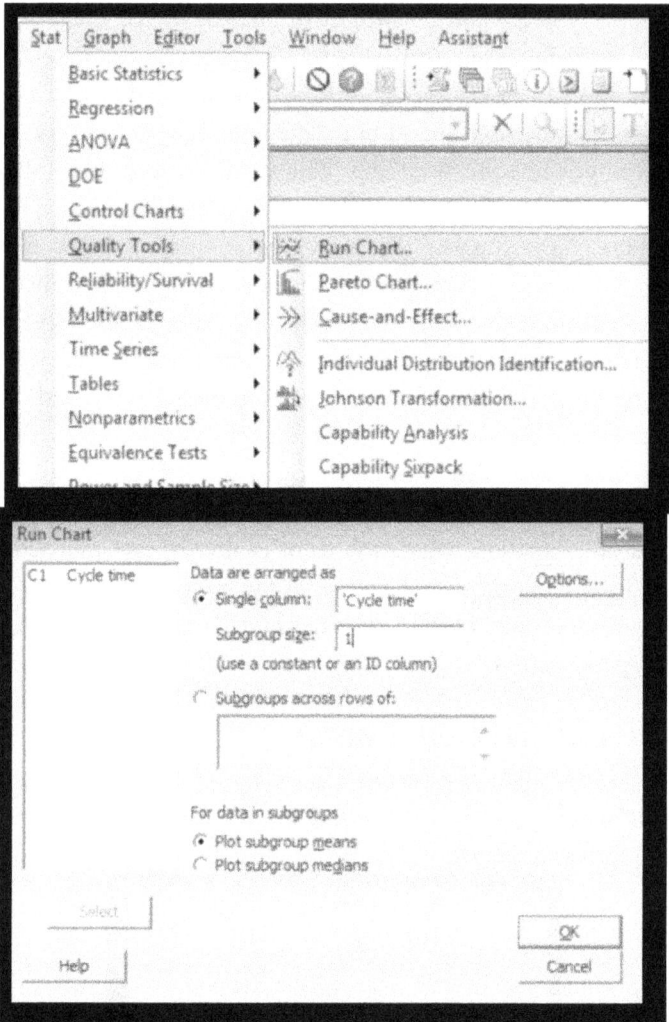

Step 3

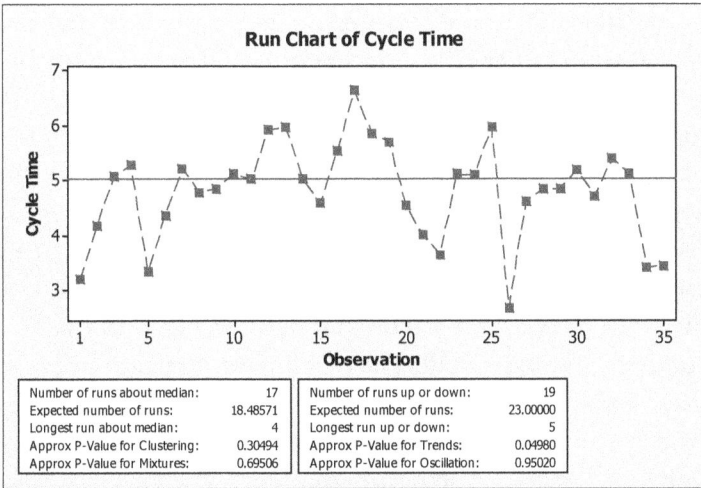

Run Chart of Cycle Time

Number of runs about median:	17	Number of runs up or down:	19
Expected number of runs:	18.48571	Expected number of runs:	23.00000
Longest run about median:	4	Longest run up or down:	5
Approx P-Value for Clustering:	0.30494	Approx P-Value for Trends:	0.04980
Approx P-Value for Mixtures:	0.69506	Approx P-Value for Oscillation:	0.95020

Clusters   – indicate sampling or measurement problems.
Mixtures   – indicate mixed data from two populations.
Oscillation – data varies up and down rapidly.
Trends   – trending of data.
P - value should be greater than 0.05 for clusters, mixtures, trends and oscillations to say that there are no special causes present in the sample data.

It is good if the data is stable (means no special cause). The concern is when you get a special cause.

What are some of the things a Black Belt should do if there are special causes present in data sets?
1. If the P-value of clusters is less than 0.05 then there is a sampling issue. Black Belt/Master Black Belt might have missed a subgroup or there is a smaller sample size considered for that data. Recommendation: Increase the sample size to a statistically validated sample size so that the data will be stable.
2. If there is an issue with the mixtures, it means there is data for two very different subgroups mixed together. Recommendation: Do subgrouping in the data or treat them separately as two different

metrics for two projects. Also, look for extreme outliers, which could be variations due to special causes. **Assign a reason and fix the special cause variation.** Remove the relevant data from the data set.

3. If there is an issue with the oscillations, it means the data is fluctuating up and down very frequently and there is huge variation in the process on a daily basis. Recommendation: Study the process and find out the reasons for the huge variations. If these are due to special causes remove some of the data points to get stability; if that outlier is part of the process, then you can't remove the outlier. Study the process more and plan for the outlier on a daily basis.

4. If there is an issue with the trends, it implies that there are too many data points either increasing or decreasing in the data set. Recommendation: Find out outliers and remove them, else study the process if it is part of another process; then increase the sample size to neutralise it.

Let's take one example to understand how the data can be made stable for the project.

The run chart for the following data is not stable as the P-value of mixtures is less than 0.05.

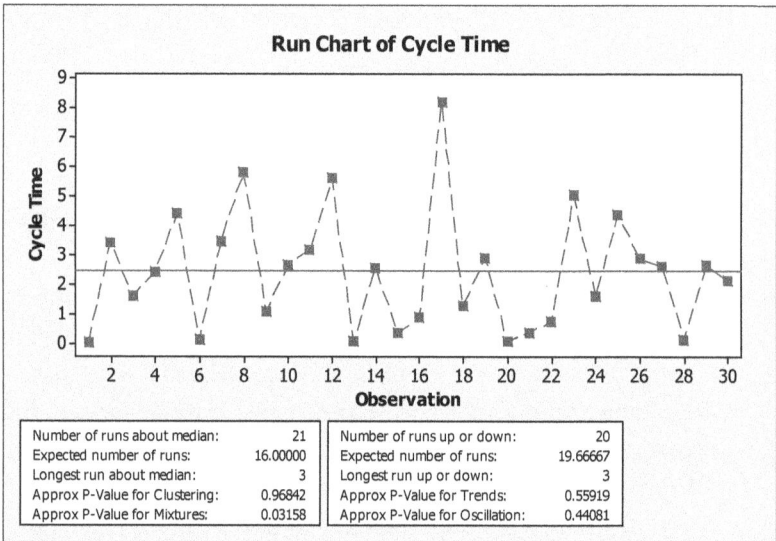

Run Chart of Cycle Time

Number of runs about median:	21	Number of runs up or down:	20
Expected number of runs:	16.00000	Expected number of runs:	19.66667
Longest run about median:	3	Longest run up or down:	3
Approx P-Value for Clustering:	0.96842	Approx P-Value for Trends:	0.55919
Approx P-Value for Mixtures:	0.03158	Approx P-Value for Oscillation:	0.44081

Cycle Time
0.0483
3.44775
1.62393
2.4099
4.45652
0.12823
3.49335
5.82082
1.10832
2.65651
3.19295
5.64284
0.06481
2.57917
0.35106
0.8829
8.19909
1.29675
2.92764
0.08013
0.3747
0.73565
5.03083
1.59198
4.40336
2.88536
2.6036
0.13879
2.64603
2.12456

Step 1: Check for outliers in the system. The tool to be used is Boxplot.

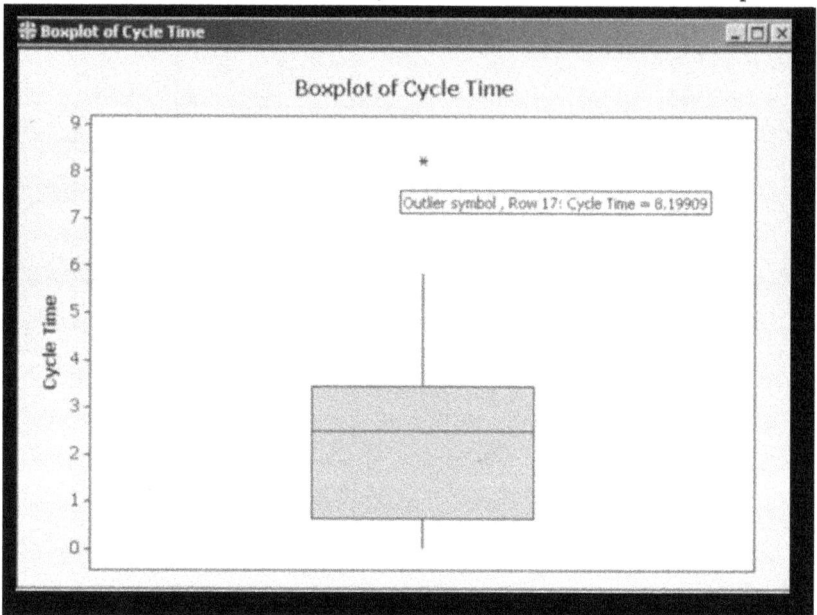

Step 2: Remove the outlier from the data set, which is row no 17, and recreate the run chart.

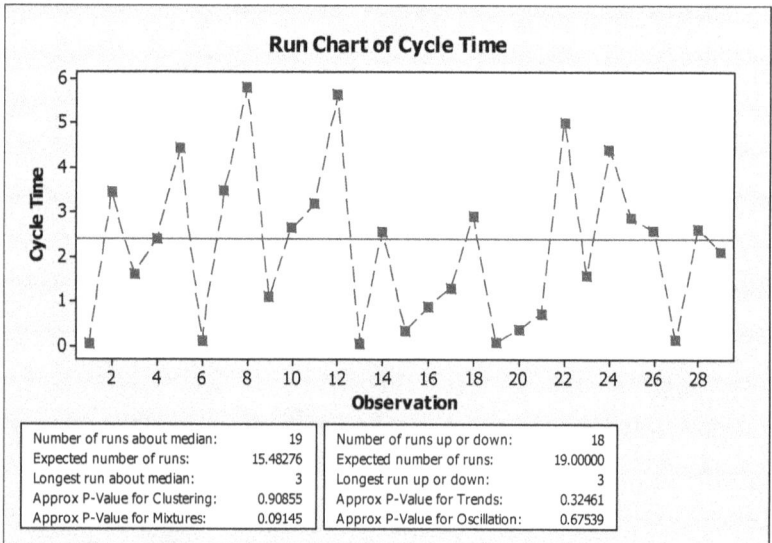

Number of runs about median:	19	Number of runs up or down:	18
Expected number of runs:	15.48276	Expected number of runs:	19.00000
Longest run about median:	3	Longest run up or down:	3
Approx P-Value for Clustering:	0.90855	Approx P-Value for Trends:	0.32461
Approx P-Value for Mixtures:	0.09145	Approx P-Value for Oscillation:	0.67539

All the P-values are greater than 0.05 now, which means the data is stable and can be used for LSS project.

Normality

When data is stable, the next step is to check the shape of the data. If data is normally distributed then a specific set of tools are used, else other sets of tools are used.

Minitab helps us identify the normality of the data.

How does one do that in Minitab?

Enter data of Y in Minitab.

Go to Stat>basic statistics and graphical summary; enter cycle time data under variable and press ok.

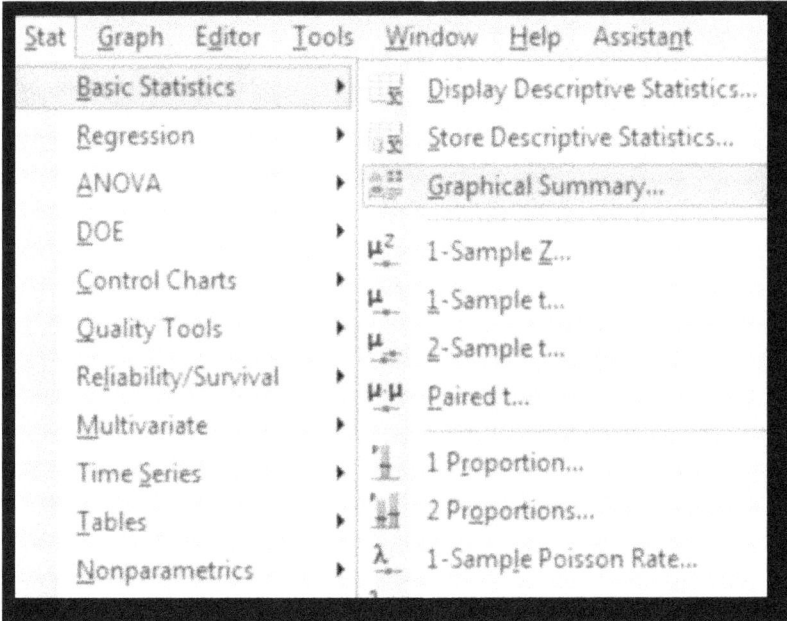

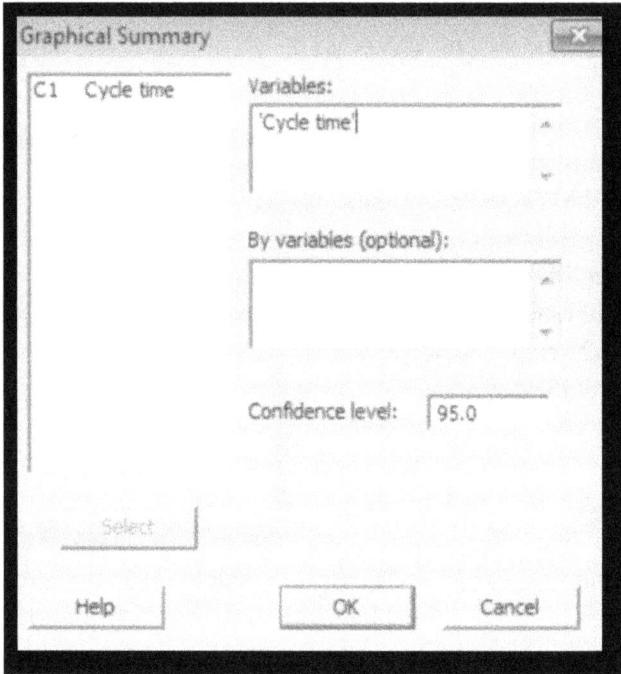

Graphical Summary

C1   Cycle time

Variables:
'Cycle time'

By variables (optional):

Confidence level: 95.0

Select

Help   OK   Cancel

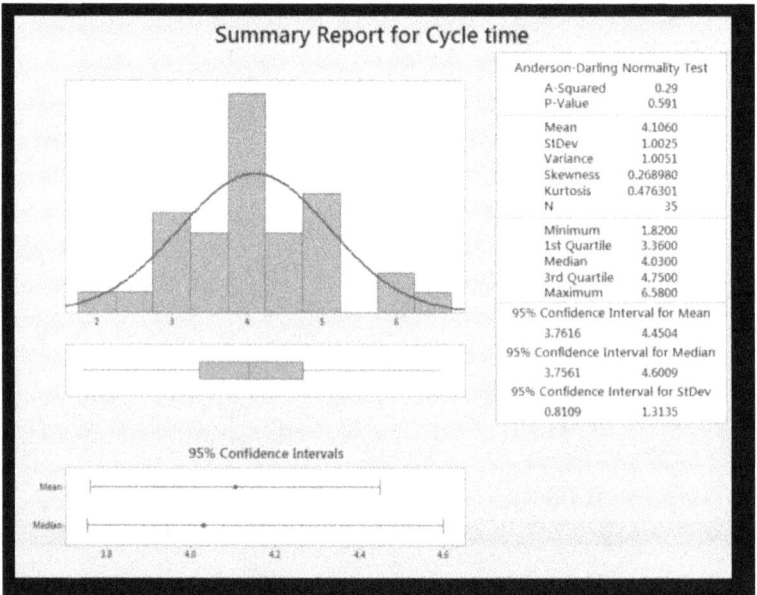

Summary Report for Cycle time

Anderson-Darling Normality Test	
A-Squared	0.29
P-Value	0.591
Mean	4.1060
StDev	1.0025
Variance	1.0051
Skewness	0.268980
Kurtosis	0.476301
N	35
Minimum	1.8200
1st Quartile	3.3600
Median	4.0300
3rd Quartile	4.7500
Maximum	6.5800

95% Confidence Interval for Mean
3.7616   4.4504
95% Confidence Interval for Median
3.7561   4.6009
95% Confidence Interval for StDev
0.8109   1.3135

95% Confidence Intervals

Mean

Median

If the P-value of the normality chart is greater than 0.05 then the data is normal, else non-normal.

If the data is normal distributed, then we use Mean and Standard deviation to define the goal statement.

If data is non-normal distributed, then we use Median and IQR to define the goal statement.

In any improvement project, a goal statement can be amended till this point only.

○ Process Capability

Process capability: This refers to the ability of a process to produce a defect-free product or service.

* You can calculate a Z-value for any given value of X.

* Z is the number of standard deviations which will fit between the mean and the value of X.

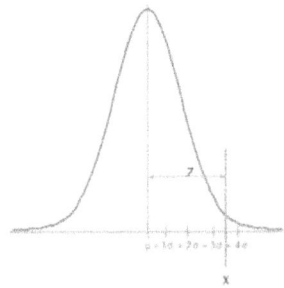

Continuous data: To calculate process capability in continuous normal data, the formula that can be used is $Z = (X - \mu) / \sigma$.

☑ The Z-score corresponds to yield, or the area under the curve inside the specification limits.

☑ The Z-value is a non-dimensional quantity that enables us to compare different processes–it represents the process capability.

Let us understand this with the help of an example:
Suppose the USL = X
then
USL = 30, Mean = 25, Standard deviation = 1
Z bench = (30-25)/1
Sigma Value =5 Sigma.

For continuous data, Minitab out can also be used.

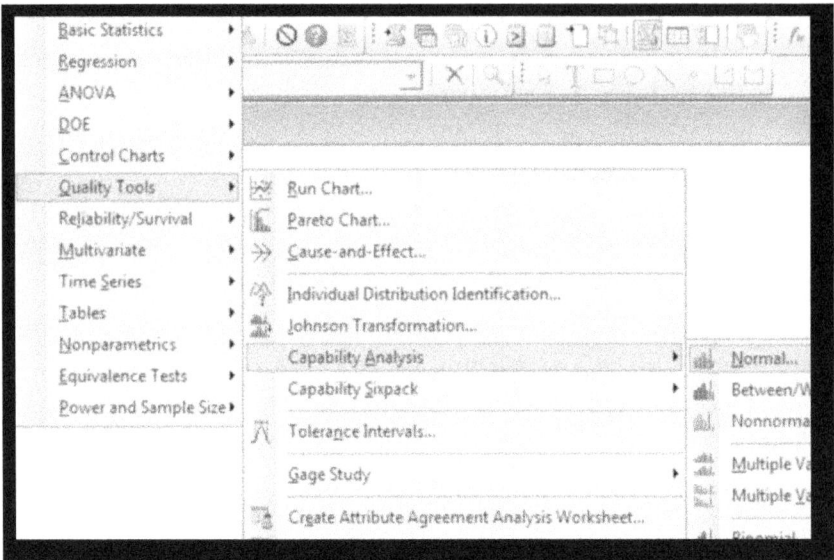

Select cycle time in Single Column. Select Subgroup Size as 1, put Upper Spec as 7 and Lower Spec as 2.

Upper Specification and Lower Specification limits are defined by the customer.

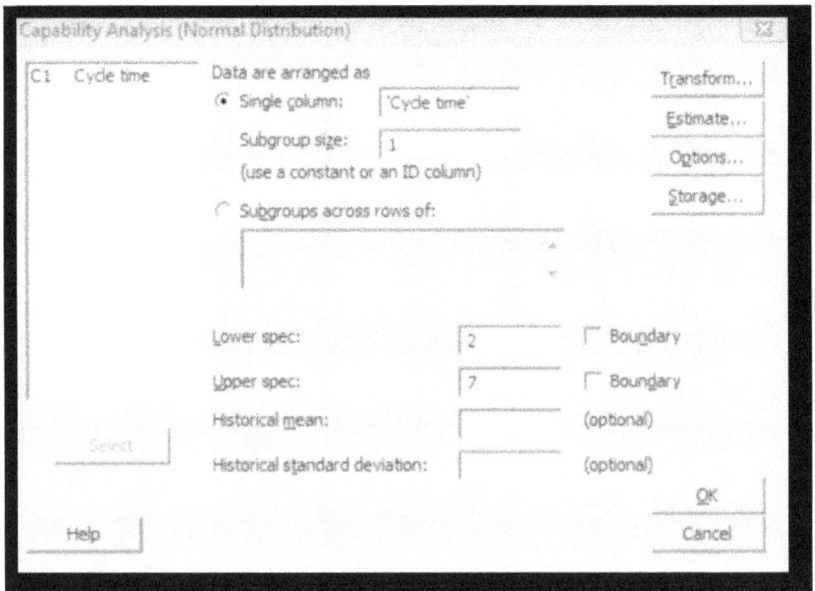

Next step: Go to Options and select Benchmark Z's (Sigma Level).

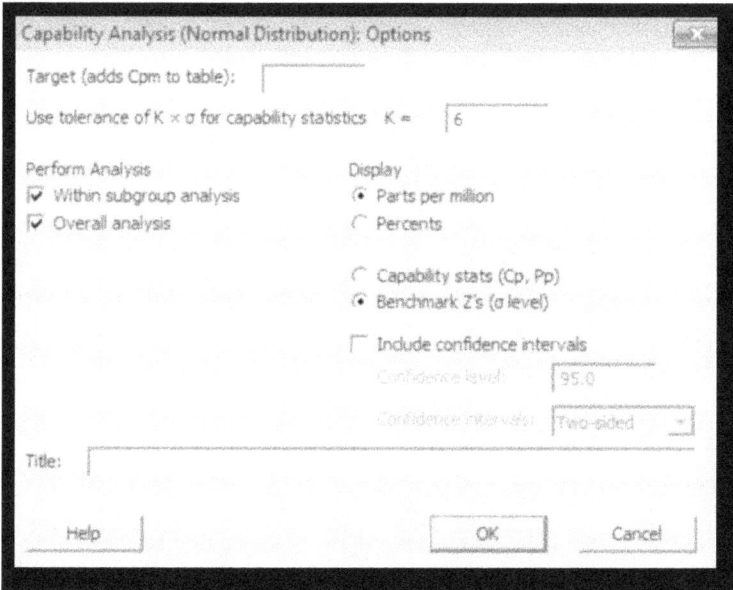

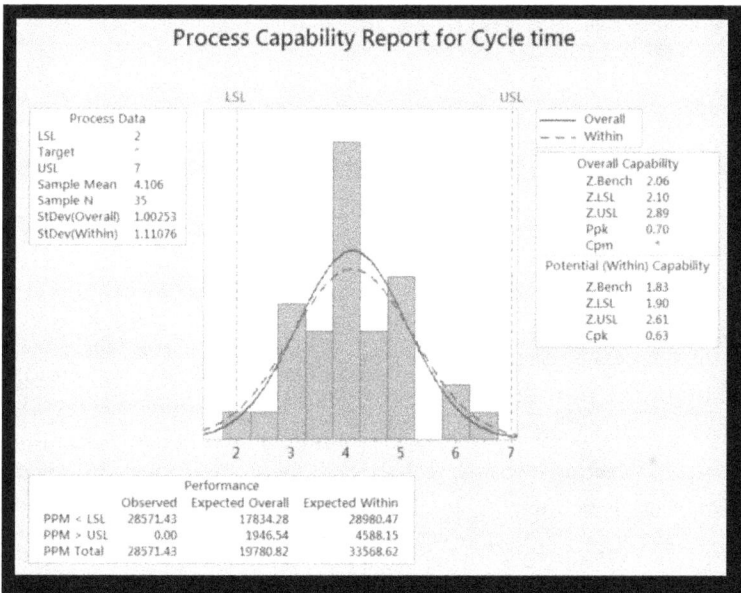

Click Ok; the graph on the right shows Z bench (process sigma) of 2.06.

For Discrete data & Non-Normal data: To calculate process capability for discrete and non-normal data, below is the formula to be used in Excel.

=normsinv (1-(total defects/total opportunities))+1.5

Total opportunities = Total Units × Opportunity per unit.

For example:

Total no. of defects – 25

Total units – 750

Opportunity per unit (there are 5 opportunities to make an error in this case) – 5

Process sigma = normsinv (1-(25/3750))+1.5 = 3.974.

Data Type	What is Capability	Tool	Example
Continuous (Normal)	Sigma Value	Minitab – Process Capability	Cycle time(P>0.05)
Continuous (Non-normal)	Median, Spans and Quartiles	Excel Formula – normsinv (1-(D/O))+1.5	Cycle time (no. of defects)
Discrete	DPMO	Excel Formula – normsinv (1-(D/O))+1.5	Accuracy

○ Data Analysis – Hypothesis Testing

Data Analysis - Above and Beyond Hypothesis Testing

A critical milestone in the journey of a Lean Six Sigma project is to perform data analysis, reach logical conclusions and provide sustainable solutions to the problems identified. Hypothesis testing is the soul of that data analysis. In this day and age of technology, systems like Minitab, Sigma Excel, etc. are readily available, and widely used data interpretation beyond the

Hypothesis testing is statistical analysis to determine if observed differences, between two or more data samples, are due to random chance or are true differences. Increases confidence of probable Xs being statistically significant.

Why hypothesis: To improve processes, we need to identify factors which impact the mean or standard deviation. Once we have identified these factors and made adjustments, we need to validate the actual improvements in our processes.

humble P-value's basis and statistical outputs have become few and far between. Apart from the statistical analysis of that data, it is also equally critical to understand what is happening within those vital lead indicators (project **inputs Xs**) which are impacting the project **output Y.**

For example, in a restaurant there is a project done by Quality Black Belt: to reduce the cycle time to place the orders by an occupied table by 30% and there is an X, which is 'number of customers' in the restaurant at any given point in time with a fixed number of waiters on the restaurant floor.

Look at the analysis below. It depicts P-value 0.00 which says that this X could impact the output Y and it is true also; as the number of customers increase, the cycle time to place the order from them to the same number of waiters will also increase. This doesn't mean that the project team will treat this X as significant and try and reduce the number of customers. Black Belts should be conscious that analysis should be beyond P-value also.

One-way ANNOVA: Cycle time to place the order versus no. of customers					
Source	DF	SS	MS	F	P
No. of customers	24	110.893	4.621	21.35	0.000
Error	10	2.165	0.216		
Total	34	113.057			
S = 0.4652 R-Sq = 98.09% R-Sq(adj) = 93.49%					

This is an attempt to help Black Belts/Master Black Belts understand life beyond P-values. If the Black Belt finds out that the Xis significant through a P-value of a hypothesis test and is not concerned about whether there is a standard deviation or mean issue, he can't provide the right solutions to the problems.

Before I start to explain it further, it is important to understand a little more about hypothesis testing.

There are two terms called Null Hypothesis and Alternate Hypothesis

Null Hypothesis (H$_o$)	Alternate Hypothesis (H$_a$)

• Usually describes a status quo
• It is the one assumed to be true until proven otherwise
• It is the one rejected based on evidence
• P-value should be greater than 0.05
• Example:
  • Data is normal
  • No difference between two samples
	• What is being proven
	• Accepted only when evidence proves it
	• P-value should be less than 0.05
	• Example:
	  • Data is non-normal
	  • Difference between two samples exists

There is a sequence that we need to follow while doing hypothesis testing.

1. Check the normality of data by using the Anderson Darling test and if the P-value of this test is greater than 0.05, then the data is normal; else it is non-normal data and you have to refer to the table below for selection of an appropriate hypothesis test.

2. First check for the difference in variation and then for the difference in the means of the variables in the Xs.

	Y Continuous - Normal	Y Continuous - Non Normal	Y Discrete
X Continuous	Simple Linear Regression		Logistic Regression
X Discrete 1 variable	1T	1 Sample Wilcoxon	1P
2 variables	2T	Mann Whitney	2P
2 or more than 2 variable	One-way Annova	Mood's Median	Chi Square
	Test for Equal Variance		

P-value:

1. Alpha is the maximum acceptable probability of being wrong if the alternate hypothesis is selected.

2. The P-value is the probability that you will be wrong if you select the alternate hypothesis.
3. Unless there is an exception based on engineering judgment, we will set an acceptance level of P at alpha = 0.05.
4. Thus, any P-value less than 0.05 means we reject the null hypothesis.

Let us consider an example to understand this well.

Example: The project is to reduce the cycle time of the transaction and I am trying to statistically prove the probability of whether people working in different shifts (morning/evening) are impacting project Y.

To check the probability of an X impacting Y, we need to first find out whether the variables within that X have differences in means or standard deviation. If mean or standard deviation or both are different between the variables of that particular X, then there is an increased probability of its greater impact on the project metric (Y). This is further explained with the help of four different cases in this example.

In this data, set Y is continuous (cycle time per transaction) and X is discrete (shift) and has two variables (morning/evening). I can use a '2T or Annova test for mean' and 'Test of equal variance for standard deviation' (precondition of checking the difference in means) and there are four outputs possible.

Case I: Mean of morning shift is equal to mean of evening shift; however, there is a difference in standard deviations (spread of data) and hence the **probability of X becoming a significant X increases.**

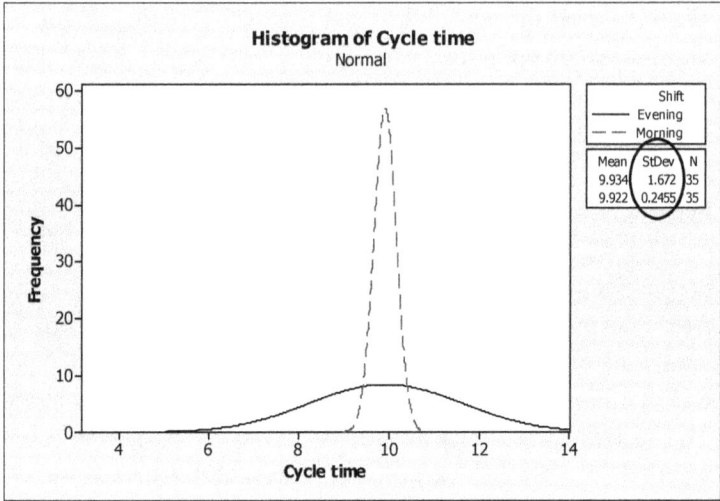

Histogram of Cycle time
Normal

	Mean	StDev	N
	9.934	1.672	35
	9.922	0.2455	35

Case II: Mean of morning shift is different from mean of evening shift; however, standard deviations (spread of data) are the same and hence **probability of X becoming a significant X increases.**

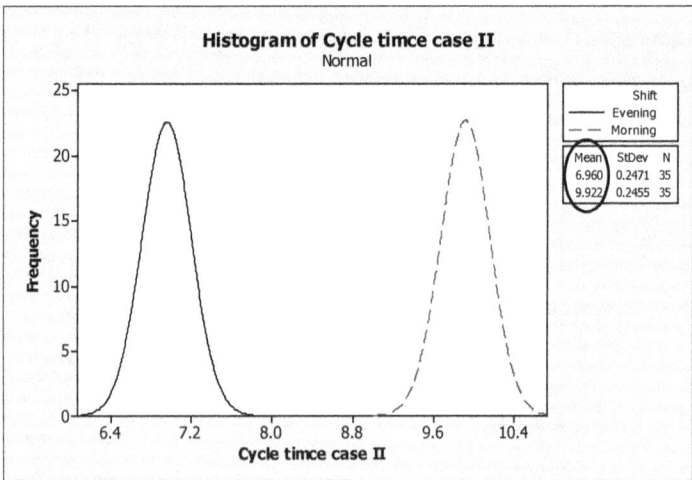

Histogram of Cycle timce case II
Normal

	Mean	StDev	N
	6.960	0.2471	35
	9.922	0.2455	35

Case III: Mean and standard deviation of the morning shift are different from mean of the evening shift and hence **probability of X becoming a significant X increases.**

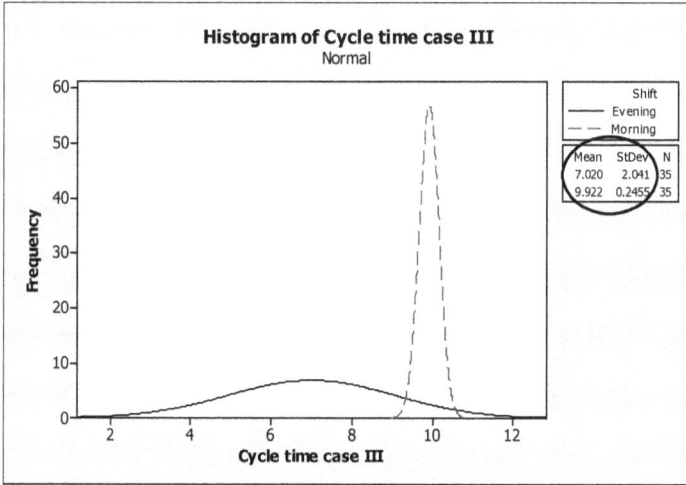

Histogram of Cycle time case III
Normal

Case IV: Mean and standard deviation of morning and evening shifts are similar and hence probability of X being **significant** goes down.

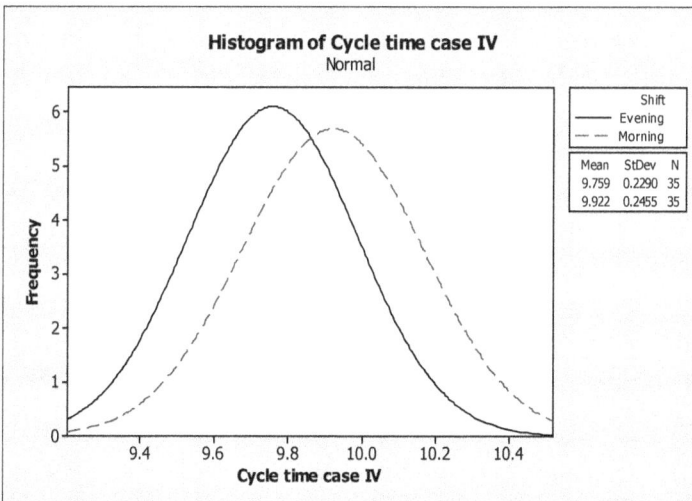

Histogram of Cycle time case IV
Normal

If the Black Belt discovers that the probability of being a **significant** X is high through a P-value of a hypothesis test and is not concerned about whether there is a standard deviation or mean issue, he can't provide the correct solutions to the problems.

Another noteworthy point is that it may well be true that means and variances are statistically not different, but that may not mean processes 'require no further action'. The Black Belt is responsible for understanding the practical, business implications of such a conclusion and act accordingly. It is not unusual to find differences that are not statistically significant because variation is high; and, with further investigation, the source of high variation is due to poor measurement systems or multiple sources of noise in the process. In fact, further actions are very much required to solve the problem.

Interpreting the result:

Let us consider all the cases discussed one by one and try and look for differences in the solutions. Remember, there could be only one situation possible out of the four at any given point in time.

Case I: This is where means are same and standard deviation is different, suggesting that in the evening shift some agents are taking more time to process transactions and some are taking less time and hence variation exists. However, if I look at the average of both shifts, it is the same for both shifts and the solution should be up-skilling (process training) the agents taking more time to process in order to reduce inter-agent variation.

Or

There is a possibility that the cycle time to process the transactions allocated in the evening shift is actually different, and we should not work on the agents taking more time to process. However, the focus should be on the right mix of transactions to be allocated in both shifts.

Both these solutions pertain to reducing the variation rather than shifting the mean. Let's understand Case II now.

Case II: When means are very different in both the shifts, it suggests that there are different skill sets available in both the shifts. It may be possible that during the evening shift, people with less tenure (0-6 months) in the process are working compared to the morning shift (greater than 6 months). So, the solution would be to mix both the batches and provide a buddy system and support in the morning shift to handle queries and help the lesser tenured associates.

Case III: Means are different and standard deviations are also different. This suggests that the process is in bad shape. It requires a deeper analysis and application of the solutions suggested in both Case I and Case II.

Case IV: Means and standard deviations are statistically same. They may look different mathematically; however, statistically they are the same and hence, require no further action.

There are some **interesting examples** to highlight the mistakes if the above-mentioned four cases are not evaluated.

Example I: In one of the transport projects, delay in the reporting time of cabs was conducted.

The data was collected for two cabs for 35 random days, each for the same route.

The data for both the cabbies are listed below:

Delay in pickup of cab A	Delay in pickup of cab B
8.84144	8.4741
8.89606	7.1027
9.32023	7.2169
9.11594	9.5740
9.38371	12.7717
9.24689	8.0856
9.05139	12.2571
9.59219	9.3195
8.60427	9.9052
9.53364	9.2061
9.71423	12.6383
8.86605	10.9170
9.54752	6.2347
9.32415	8.6483
9.21725	6.0609
9.34818	6.7322
9.47320	6.9182
9.25756	8.6122
9.48943	8.1147
9.01005	9.9092
9.68938	8.2533
9.17567	14.7043
9.43301	9.8916
9.59798	4.9458
9.38270	9.7673
9.47824	9.4897
9.15113	6.5099
9.71861	9.8320
9.00879	11.6943
9.12036	14.1272
9.49672	9.1190
9.49237	10.7504
9.56375	10.7390
9.18543	7.4158
9.39850	10.8019

Step 1: Checking normality shows the data is normal for both the cabs.

Step 2: Check for central tendencies issues and 2 T test can be conducted to see the statistical difference.

Null & Alternate Hypothesis Conditions:
Ho: mu (cab A) = mu (cab B)
Ha: mu (cab A) ≠ mu (cab B)

Two-Sample T-Test and CI: Delay Cycle Time, Cab

Two-Sample T for delay cycle time

Cab	N	Mean	St Dev	SE Mean
A	35	9.306	0.270	0.046
B	35	9.34	2.29	0.39

Difference = mu (A) - mu (B)
Estimate for difference: -0.028980
95% CI for difference: (-0.820629, 0.762669)
T-Test of difference = 0 (vs not =): T-value = -0.07 P-value = 0.941 DF = 34

Result: A P-value of greater than 0.05 suggests that we fail to reject Ho, which suggests the mean of both the cabs are similar and the cabbie is not the significant contributor to employee dissatisfaction. In this situation, we have rejected Case II and Case III.

Note: It would have been our biggest mistake if we had not checked the variations between the two cabbies, (which are to test for Case I and IV from the earlier-mentioned cases).

Step 3: Variation Study. What happens when variation is checked? The statistical test used here is 'Test for Equal Variance'.

Null & Alternate Hypothesis Conditions:
Ho: Eta cab A = Eta cab B
Ha: Eta cab A ≠ Eta cab B

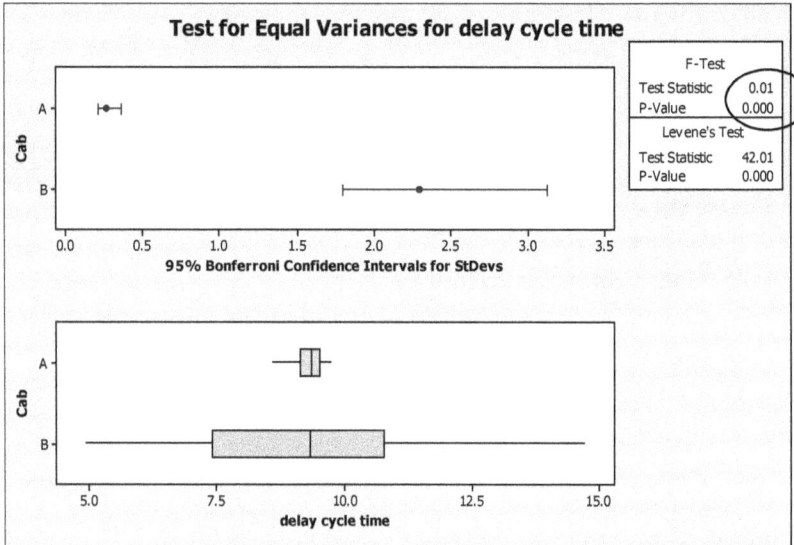

Result: The P-value of F test is less than 0.05 and hence, Ho is rejected. The analysis is that there is huge variation in the two data sets and hence we should consider the cabbie as a huge probability of being critical to employee satisfaction and do further root cause analysis.

Final Outcome: In the above-mentioned four cases, Case I is true here. The cabbie could be critical and needs to be analysed further for the success of the project.

Example 2: In one of the claim processing accounts, a project was done to reduce the claim processing cycle time and was studied with respect to the type of claims.

Below is the cycle time data to process both types of claims:

Claim Type A	Claim Type B
15.4562	11.3864
14.7352	10.2908
16.1209	13.2711
16.7266	12.6429
14.5161	9.5693
13.7743	10.3714
15.6769	12.8333
15.3577	13.7605
14.3978	11.7092
15.4341	12.1117
16.0064	11.3443
15.2166	12.3856
15.9808	11.0977
16.1431	10.8958
14.5019	12.2608
14.0966	11.9942
14.5604	11.8709
15.2194	11.2739
14.7103	11.2057
16.0595	12.0139
14.6529	12.4751
15.4414	10.9491
15.251	10.8363
15.6041	12.0909
15.441	11.6385
14.8748	12.6809
14.2776	12.4861
15.717	12.6442
14.6678	11.6926
13.8605	12.12
15.4051	12.785
17.0643	10.6778
15.171	11.2237
14.222	12.1745
15.4111	13.3768

All the above four cases were tested and listed below are the results.

Variation Study: The data of both the variables is normally distributed within the X (claim type); hence F Test's P-value has been studied under a test of equal variance.

Null & Alternate Hypothesis Conditions:
Ho: variances are the same
Ha: variances are not the same

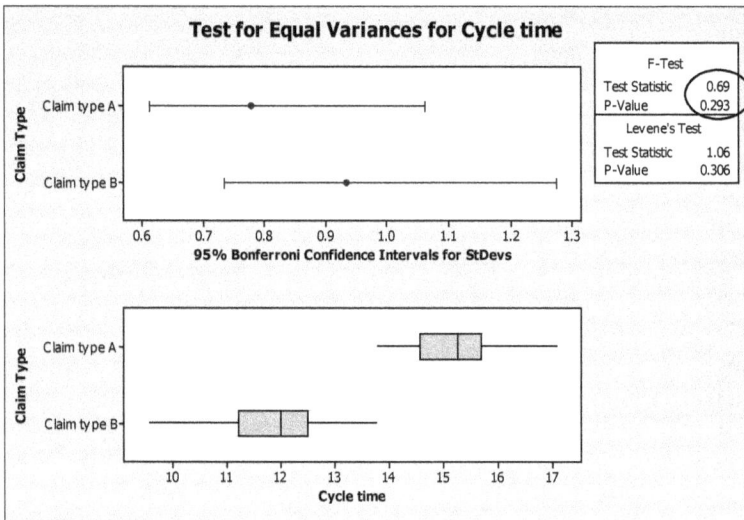

Result: A P-value of greater than 0.05 suggests Ho is accepted, which means X is impacting project Y significantly and hence no action is required. Case I and III are rejected.

Note: Now we would have made a same similar error, as was highlighted in Example 1, if we would have stopped our analysis at this point.

Mean/Median Study: The data of both the variables is normally distributed within the X (claim type); hence two-sample T test is used. The result is listed below.

Null and Alternate Hypothesis:
Ho: mu (Claim type A) = mu (Claim type B)
Ha: mu (Claim type A) ≠ mu (Claim type B)

Two-Sample T-Test and CI: Claim type A, Claim type B

Two-Sample T for Claim type A vs Claim type B

N Mean St Dev SE Mean
Claim type A 35 15.193 0.778 0.13
Claim type B 35 11.833 0.933 0.16

Difference = mu (Claim type A) - mu (Claim type B)
Estimate for difference: 3.36033
95% CI for difference: (2.95036, 3.77031)
T-Test of difference = 0 (vs not =): T-Value = 16.37 P-Value = 0.000 DF = 65

Result: A P-value of less than 0.05 suggests Ho is rejected and hence X can impact project Y significantly. This indicates that we should do RCA on why the claim type is impacting cycle time to process the claims.

Final Outcome: In the above-mentioned four cases, Case II is true here and the claim type is a significant X.

Black Belts are sometimes confused on what null and alternate hypothesis tests are while performing different hypothesis tests. For a quick orientation, they can refer to the table below.

Mean	Median	Proportions	Standard Deviation
1 Sample t-test	One Sample Wilcoxon test	1P	Test for equal variance
H_o mu1 = mu historic	H_o mdn 1 = mdn Historic	H_o P1=Historic Proportion	H_o ■1 = ■2
H_a mu1 # mu historic	H_a mdn 1 # mdn Historic	H_a P1#Historic Proportion	H_a ■1 # ■2
Two Sample t-test, ANOVA	Mann-Whitney, test, Mood's Median	2P and Chi square	
H_o mu1 = mu2	H_o mdn 1 = mdn 2	H_o P1 = P	
H_a mu1# mu2	H_a mdn 1 # mdn 2	H_a P1 # P	

Moral of the story: Black Belts should continue using hypothesis tests and looking at the significant P-values of those tests. However, they need to go one step further and dive deep into what the cause of that significance is and thereby provide real impact solutions which could deliver customer delight. This chapter is the key to success for this.

Minitab path for some of the hypotheses tests:
1. 1 Way Annova: Stat >> Annova >> One way
2. Test for Equal Variance: Stat >> Annova >> Test for Equal Variance
3. Mood's Median Test: Stat >> Nonparametrics >> Moods Median Test
4. Chi-Square Test for Association: Stat >> Tables >> Chi-square Test for Association
5. Simple Linear Regression: Stat >> Regression>> Fitted line plot

Minitab's 'Help' function can be used to further learn about how to perform these tests

In a Six Sigma project, there are times when data can't be collected on all the Xs (Potential Causes); the rest of the potential causes are to be dealt by the process door approach.

Before a Black Belt starts finding solutions for all data and process door Xs, they need to identify significant Xs from process door Xs as well. For data door Xs, 'Hypothesis Testing' is used and for Process door, 'Nominal Group Technique' can be used to identify significant Xs.

The **nominal group technique** (**NGT**) is a group process involving problem identification, solution generation, and decision making. It can be used in groups where everyone's opinions are taken into account (as opposed to traditional voting, where only the largest group is considered). The method of tallying is the difference. First, every member of the group gives their views on identified process door causes (Xs), with short explanations. Then, duplicate causes (Xs) are eliminated from the list, and the members proceed to rank the causes, 1st, 2nd, 3rd, 4th, and so on.

The sum all the ranks given by individuals of the potential Xs need to be considered; then. The Black Belt needs to pick the top one or two Xs to find solutions.

For example :

Process Door Xs	Person1	Person2	Person3	Rank
System Issues	1	1	2	4
Network Down Time	3	4	3	10
Lengthy Forms	2	2	1	5
Batch Processing	4	3	4	11
Laggy User Interface	5	5	5	15

In the example above, 'System Issues' and 'Lengthy Forms' are the significant Xs from process door.

REFER TO THE CASE STUDY AND CREATE THE ABOVE STEPS

Create a run chart of the cycle time data. If the P-values of clusters, mixtures, oscillations and trends are greater than 0.05, then the data is stable and has no special causes. This data can be further analysed to find out the root causes.

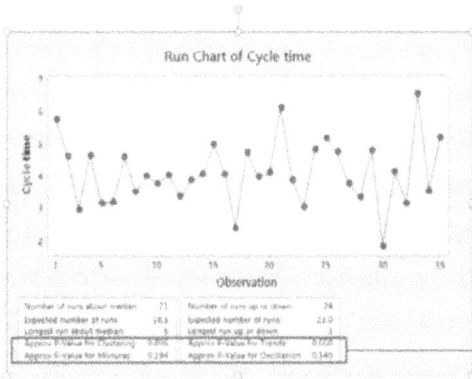

To find out data normality, run a graphical summary report.

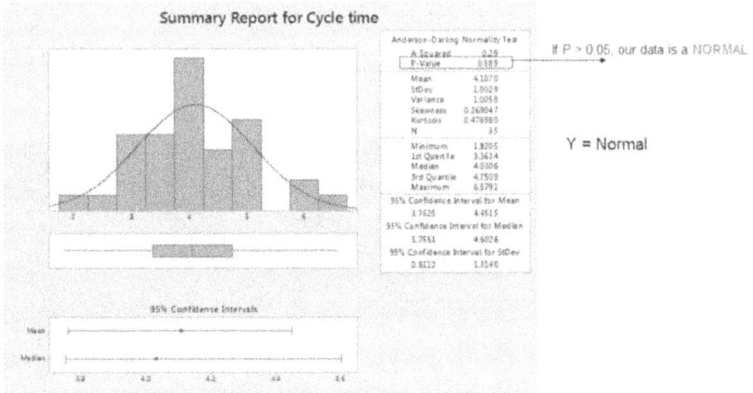

Summary Report for Cycle time

Run process capability report for normal data.

Process Capability refers to the ability of a process to produce a defect-free product or service for

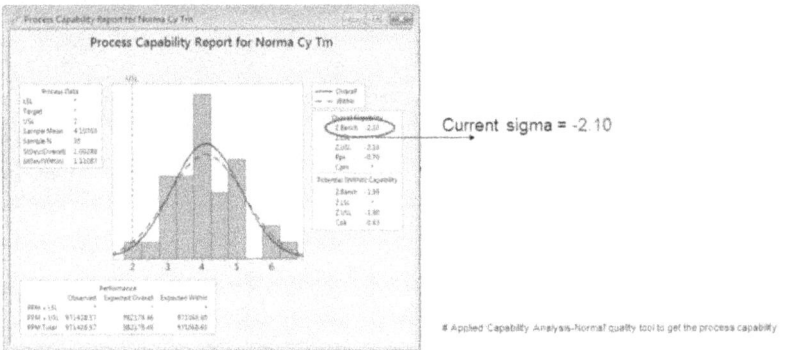

Process Capability Report for Norma Cy Tm

Start identifying significant Xs by using hypothesis testing. Since Y is normal and Xs are discrete, one needs to test for equal variance and one way Annova tests would be used. Both are required to check the variation or mean problems.

One of the data door Xs is continuous; simple linear regression is used to check the correlation of X with Project Y.

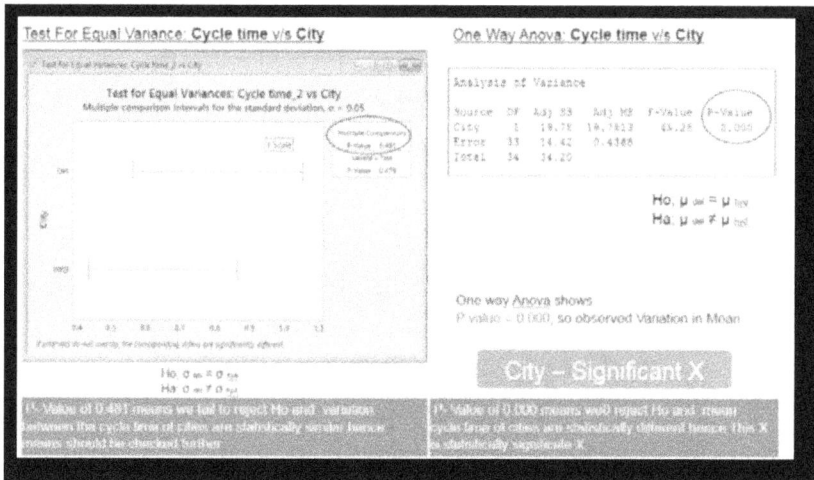

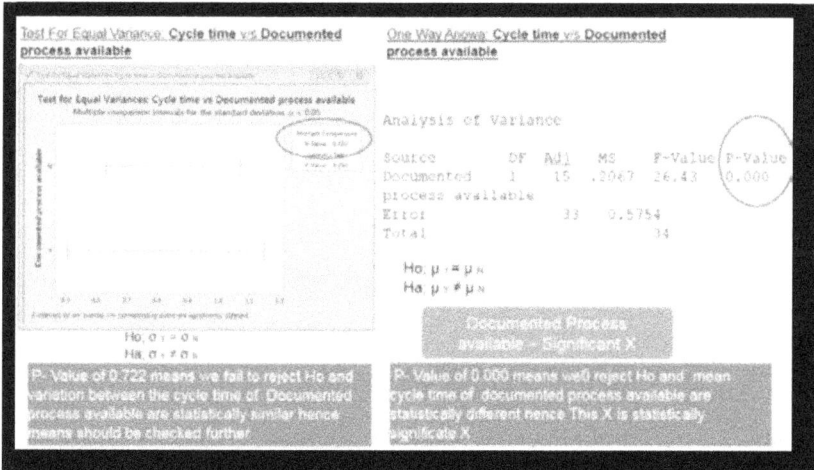

For the rest of the discrete X, the same process is to be followed.

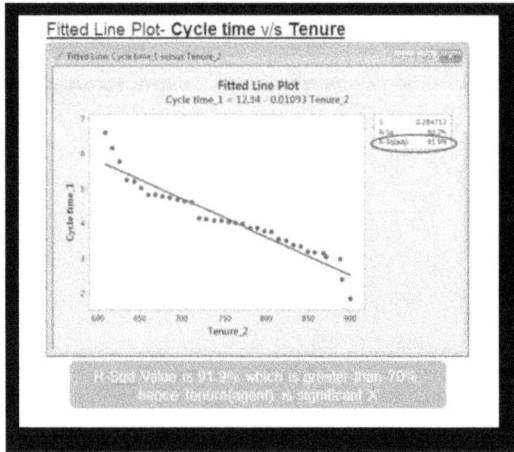

Y	Data Type	X	Data Type	Hypothesis Test		Result
Cycle time	Continuous	City	Discrete	Annova	Test for equal variance	Significant
		Shift	Discrete	Annova	Test for equal variance	Non-Significant
		Documented process available	Discrete	Annova	Test for equal variance	Significant
		Agent	Discrete	Annova	Test for equal variance	Non-Significant
		Branch	Discrete	Annova	Test for equal variance	Significant
		Tenure	Continuous	Simple Linear Regression		Significant
		Week of the month	Discrete	Annova	Test for equal variance	Significant

Questions for the 'analyse' phase

Q1. What is a run chart? Define its significance.

Q2. What is the P-value in a normality chart to indicate the data is normal?

Q3. What is P and what is α?

Q4. For each scenario described below, which hypothesis testing tool would you use? Assume normal distribution where appropriate

- A Six Sigma project is being conducted to improve the cycle time for report generation. Report generation times were measured for a period of six weeks for four regions. The Green Belt suspects that there is a difference in average report generation times among each of the regions. How would you test whether there is a statistically significant difference in mean cycle time for the different regions?

- A Six Sigma project is being conducted to increase the accuracy of payroll processing. A Green Belt on the project believes payroll errors are contributed by time card errors which vary across business units. Time card error data is recorded for 150 employees spanning all the business units. How would you test if there is a statistically significant difference in the number of errors between the different business units?

- A Black Belt project team is trying to reduce the processing time for journals during the month-end close process to close the ledger on workday 3. After a few workshops, the team believes that there is a huge amount of processing time variation between the different decision support groups. How will the team confirm this finding statistically?

- An HR team trying to reduce the attrition levels of employees believes that the average touch time of a manager with his/her direct reports significantly contributes to the length of service of the employee. How should the team prove that their understanding is correct?

○ Identifying Solutions

In order to identify the right solutions, identification of the correct root cause is important. There are two ways to identify the right root cause for the significant Xs.

1. Process door
2. Data door.

Tools used for Process door: Fishbone & 5 Why Analysis
Tools used for Data door: Pareto and Box Plots.

Process Door Approach:
5 why analysis

Start asking why five times to reach the actionable root cause of the particular problem.

This is a very powerful tool to identify the right root causes and solutions.

As the name of the tool is 5 why, the why is to be asked five times. However, this number can vary as per need. For example, if the right cause is identified at the 4th why, the project owner must stop; if the right root cause can't be identified even at the 5th why, the questioning can go up to 7th why.

Example of 5 why analysis
Problem: Coming late to office

Why 1	Why2	Why 3	Why 4	Why 5
Q1 Why are you late? A1 I met with an accident.	Q2 Why did you meet with an accident? A2 I was driving very fast.	Q3 Why were you driving so fast? A3 I had a fight with my wife.	Q4 Why did you fight with your wife? A4 I could not get up in the morning to get the milk.	Q5 Why could you not get up? A5 My alarm clock is faulty.

So in order to reach office in time, the person has to get his alarm clock repaired or replaced.

There could be a temptation to stop at an intermediate root cause that could lead the project owner to take incorrect decisions. The project owner must stop at the root cause which is actionable and viable.

Data Door stratification through Pareto:

Pareto is also called the 80/20 rule. 80% of the problems are due to 20% of the causes. Pareto is a tool used to stratify discrete information.

For example: In an engineering defect reduction project, the engineer is a significant X. A Pareto chart helps in the identification of 20% of the engineers producing 80% of the defects. A further second level of Pareto can help identify the types of errors made by the top 20% contributing engineers and then an action plan is created to improve those 20% engineers who make 80% of the errors.

S.No.	Engineer	Defect
1	ABC	16
2	BCD	12
3	CDE	22
4	DEF	45
5	EFG	9
6	FGH	44
7	GHI	8
8	HIJ	65
9	IJK	78
10	JKL	5

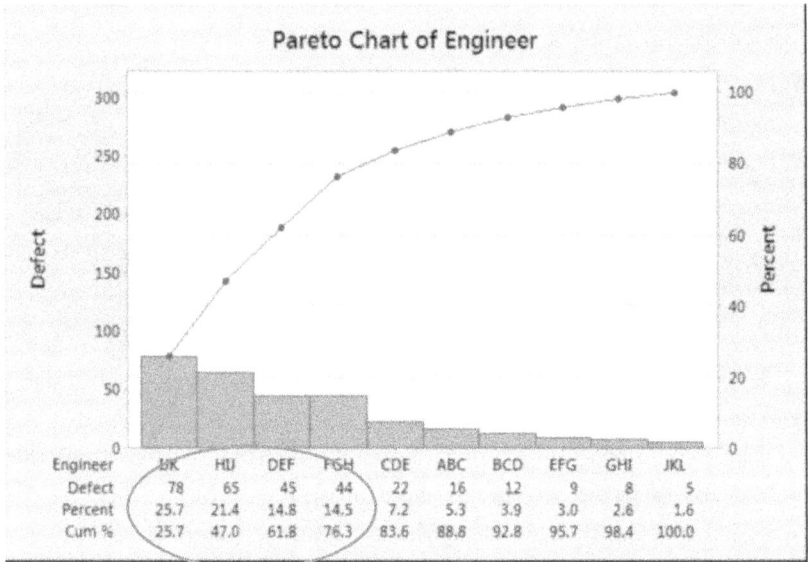

Pareto Chart of Engineer

Engineer	IJK	HIJ	DEF	FGH	CDE	ABC	BCD	EFG	GHI	JKL
Defect	78	65	45	44	22	16	12	9	8	5
Percent	25.7	21.4	14.8	14.5	7.2	5.3	3.9	3.0	2.6	1.6
Cum %	25.7	47.0	61.8	76.3	83.6	88.8	92.8	95.7	98.4	100.0

According to this Pareto chart, 76.3% of the defects are contributed by just four engineers. Further stratification is done on 232 errors made by the four engineers.

S. No.	Error Type	Count of Error
1	AB	45
2	BC	32
3	CD	56
4	EF	7
5	GH	8
6	IJ	4
7	JK	12
8	KL	13
9	LM	13
10	MN	2

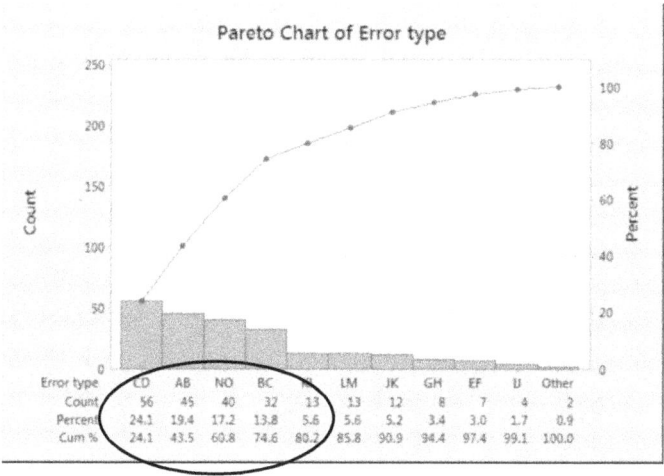

Pareto Chart of Error type

Error type	CD	AB	NO	BC	JH	LM	JK	GH	EF	IJ	Other
Count	56	45	40	32	13	13	12	8	7	4	2
Percent	24.1	19.4	17.2	13.8	5.6	5.6	5.2	3.4	3.0	1.7	0.9
Cum %	24.1	43.5	60.8	74.6	80.2	85.8	90.9	94.4	97.4	99.1	100.0

Conclusion: Error Types CD, AB, NO and BC contribute 74.6% of the errors, so further training plans and improvements should be designed for the top four error-making engineers and for the top four error categories made by them.

So, Pareto has helped in data stratification and identifying the right root cause.

Box Plot: This is a tool which helps in pictorial representation of continuous data. It can help in data stratification.

For example: A team is working on a project to improve the cycle time of the account set up process, and processes done in a different city is a **significant** X. The different cities have two shifts so stratification at level 2 can be done by a box plot.

Cycle time	City	Shift
2.93941	a	M
4.96486	c	M
2.97703	b	M
3.39805	b	M
4.31625	c	M
2.92974	a	M
0.65469	a	M

3.19642	b	M
3.24510	b	M
3.24775	b	M
3.58279	b	M
4.78755	c	M
4.17789	c	M
2.57801	a	M
1.37671	a	M
4.28113	c	M
4.97657	c	M
3.64804	b	E
3.94966	b	E
4.19044	c	E
2.62107	a	E
3.32026	b	E
4.43897	c	E
3.83318	b	E
4.26258	c	E
2.20035	a	E
3.38688	b	E
4.47510	c	E
3.43795	b	E
2.31731	a	E
2.99273	b	E
3.77452	b	E
4.50150	c	E
3.62729	b	E

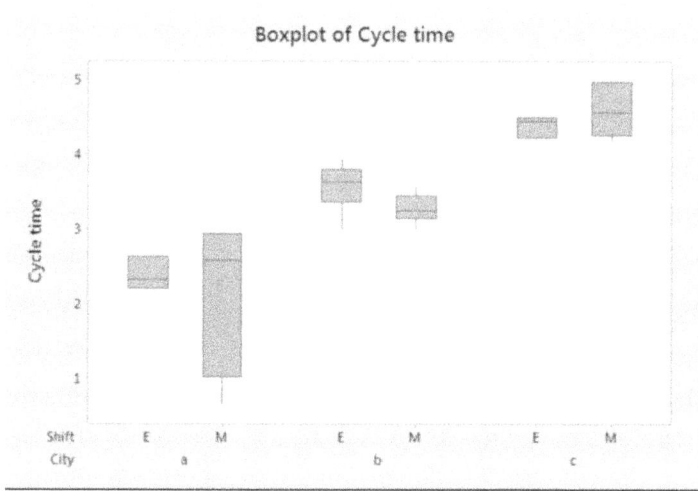

Boxplot of Cycle time

Conclusion: The 'E' shift of city 'a' has the minimum cycle time to open the account. Hence, best practices from this shift should be implemented in other cities and their shifts.

o   Prioritise the Solutions

There are various tools available to prioritise the solutions. One of them is Cause and Effect Matrix.

Cause and Effect Matrix: This tool helps decide which of the solutions identified should be addressed or implemented first.

Solution	Ease of implementation 8 ↑	Impact of idea 10 ↑	Cost of implementation 9 ↓	Total
Equal work distribution	9	9	9	253
Incentive program	3	9	3	141

In the diagram above, factors like ease of implementation, impact of idea and cost of implementation are given by the customer. The rating scale of 8, 10 and 9 is also decided by customers as per their priorities. For some customers, cost (spending money to implement a solution) is not a problem; they would rate cost lower than ease of implementation and impact generated.

The upward arrow represents higher the better and the downward arrow represents lower the better. For example, if the idea is easy to implement then a higher score is to be given. If less cost is required, then a higher score is to be allocated.

For rating the solutions, a scale of 1, 3 and 9 is used, 1 being no relation and 9 being the strongest relation.

In the above example, 'Equal work distribution' suggests it is easy to implement this solution; the impact is high and the cost is very less. So 9 is given in all the columns.

For 'Incentive program' some approvals from management are required so it is not that easy, hence a score of 3 under 'ease'. The impact would be high, so a score of 9, and 'cost' would be more as compared to 'equal work distribution', so a score of 3 is given.

Equal work distribution is prioritised for implementation; however, before implementation, all failure modes need to be checked.

o   Identify Failure Modes and Apply Mitigates

It is important to identify failure modes of the newly-identified solutions before they are implemented in the process. The tool that can be used for this is FMEA.

FMEA stands for Failure Mode and Effect Analysis.

Failure modes are any errors or defects in a process, design or item, especially those that affect the customer; they can be potential or actual.

Effect Analysis refers to studying the consequences of those failures.

Solution Step	Potential Failure Mode	Severity	Occur -rence	Detection	RPN	Mitigates
Equal Work Distribution	People with higher cycle time may miss on SLA	9	2	2 (there is a work allocation tool which can track the SLA)	36	Not required

There is a predefined scale on which severity, occurrence and detection has to be rated.

If the failure mode is very severe, like it can cause injury or death to an employee or customer, then it should be rated 10.

Severity: Missing a service level agreement for a BPO could be severe enough to be rated 9.

Occurrence: This means how many times the SLA got missed due to this new idea getting implemented, so chances are less as people are tenured enough. It has a similar cycle time to process the transaction, hence a lower score of 2 is given.

Detection: This has to be inversely proportional, which means the more you are able to detect the defect before it occurs, the lesser the score. In the above example, there is a tool to track and identify the SLA misses, hence a lesser score is given on detection.

RPN: RPN is the multiplication of SXOXD. If this number is greater than 100, then mitigate is to be applied before the solution is finally implemented in the process. If this number is less than 100, like in the example above, then the solution can be implemented immediately.

o   Implementing the Solution

After all the failure modes are checked and the RPN number is under 100 for them, then the solutions are implemented. The tool that can be used for this is 4W1H.

4W1H: What/When/Where/Who and How

What is to be implemented	When it is to be implemented	Where it is to be implemented	Who will implement	How it will be implemented
Equal work distribution	At the start of each shift	In the work allocation tool	Team leader	Use first in the first out method and ensure equal work distribution for all

This tool will help create an action plan for all the actionable solutions.

REFER TO THE CASE STUDY AND CREATE THE ABOVE STEPS
5 Why's: Identifying a solution to **significant** Xs

Significant X	Why 1	Why 2	Why 3	Solution
Branch	Branch Infrastructure	Outdated hardware	Due to cost pressures	Update hardware
		Lack of No. of branches		Open new branches
	Employees	Non-skilled employees	Hiring issues Training	• Improve hiring process • Create refresher training plan
		Lack of motivation	No. additional perks rewards & recognition	• Incentive program • Quarterly rewards & recognition

Tenure of agents	Agents with less tenure take high TAT	New agents have a lot of process queries		• Train agents on all scenarios • Enhance the training plan for new joiners
Documented process available	Some processes do not have process documents	Not there from the beginning of the process		Create process documents for all the processes
Week of month	High volume at month end	Team not cross-trained to help		Cross-train other teams to help in peak times

Some extra solutions would come from process door Xs. All the solutions are prioritised on Ease, Impact and Cost metrics. If it is easy to implement, give a high score. If the impact is high, give a high score and if the cost of implementation is low then give a high score. Rating scale – 1: less, 3: moderate, 9: high

Solution	Ease (8)↑	Impact (10)↑	Cost (8)↓	Total	Priority
Update hardware	3	3	1	24+30+8= 62	Skip
Open new branches	3	9	1	122	P4
Improve hiring process	3	9	3	138	P3
Create refresher training plan	3	3	9	126	P4
Incentive program	9	3	3	126	P4
Quarterly rewards & recognition	9	3	9	174	P2
Train agents on all scenarios	9	9	9	234	P1
Enhance the training plan for new employees	9	9	9	234	P1
Create process documents for all the processes	9	9	9	234	P1
Cross-train other teams to help in peak times	3	9	3	138	P3
Equal work distribution	9	9	9	234	P1

Perform FMEA before the solutions are implemented. It is important to find out failure modes of the solutions and put mitigates in place before they are implemented. Use the general scale available to measure Severity (Sev), Occurrence (Occ) and Detection (Det). FMEA is shown for P1 priority solutions and the rest could be made following the same guidelines.

Solution step	Potential failure mode	Potential effect of the failure	Se v	Potential cause of failure	O c c	Current process control	D e t	RPN	Recommend ed action
Equal work distribution	Not able to allocate equally and there are misses	A few employees have a heavier work load	6	No work flow tool and ad-hoc requests	8	No current control	7	336	Create an automated work allocation tool to prioritise & allocate
Create process documents for all the processes	Process documents not authenti-cated	Wrong processing on transactio ns by associates	9	Process documents not validated by customer organisation	6	No current control	7	378	Create a process to get the documents validated by customers and set up periodic review of all the documents to keep then updated
Enhance the training plan for new employees	Not all scenarios are covered	New employees will make mistakes and ask lots of questions	8	Training document is not validated by process SMEs	6	No current process	7	336	Enhance training plan of the new employees and get it validated by SMEs before every new batch
Train existing agents on all scenarios	Knowledge issue	Errors and lot of queries	8	Associates not trained properly	6	No current control	7	336	Create a training plan on all uncovered scenarios and train

Questions for 'Improve' phase

Q1. If Sev – 5 Occ -7, RPN – 175, what is the value of Det in the FMEA tool?

Q2. Post FMEA and post putting the mitigates in place, is it possible to change the Sev of the failure mode?

Q3. Which tool is used to identify root causes and solutions from the Significant Xs?

o Check Result

Keep checking the result post all the improvements that have been done. Create pre-post comparison charts and perform hypothesis tests once again to prove that the achieved target is statistically significant.

Hypothesis tests must be chosen as per the table shared earlier in the analyse phase.

o Control Plan

The biggest differentiator between an improvement initiative and a Lean Six Sigma process improvement initiative is the robustness of the control phase and how strong the controls are so that problem does not surface again. A control plan is a critical tool which plays a key role in the success of this phase.

Control Plan: It also a document that helps to keep the improved process at its current level. This is also important as it helps to keep the improved process under control.

It is a detailed document which has 4W1H, frequency of check and checked by. See the template below:

What is to be implemented	Where it is to be implemented	Who will implement	By When	How it is to implemented	Frequency of check	Checked by
Equal work distribution	Work flow tool	Team leader	Monday, 26 March	Use first in first out method and ensure equal work distribution to all	Every week	Team manager

It is important to check whatever has been decided to be implemented before it is actually implemented. If it is not checked, there is a possibility of lapses and the process may go out of control.

○ Control Chart

Control Chart

Control chart is a tool which allows a simple detection of events that are indicative of the actual process change.

This chapter will explain with live examples and thus guide all quality practitioners (Master Black Belts/Black Belts) understand and select the right control chart for situations that may arise.

The chapter will cover the following:
1. Definition and type of control charts.
2. Understanding the application of control charts with live examples from the service industry.

Definition:

A control chart is a statistical tool used to determine if a manufacturing set up or a services business is in a state of statistical control. A control chart is a type of run chart with control limits and these control limits are at +–3 standard deviation from the centre line.

There are two types of variations that exist in any process: one is common cause variation and the other is special cause variation. When only common cause variation exists in the process, then the data does not show any trends; however if any data point/points have crossed the control limits or show a systematic pattern then there is a probability of special causes being present in the process. In any Lean Six Sigma project, the data used for analysis or suggesting improvements should be freed from special causes (not in control).

Types of Control Charts

There are different types of control charts and a control chart should be selected based on the data type (continuous/discrete).

For continuous data, there are three control charts and for discrete there are four.

S. No.	Continuous Data	Discrete Data
1	IMR	C
2	X Bar R	U
3	X Bar S	P
4		Np

In continuous data, a control chart is selected depending on the subgroup size.

Description	Control Chart
Sample is individual measurement. Subgroup size is one.	IMR (individual moving range)
Sample is subgroup averages with subgroup sizes. Sub group size is 2-8	X bar R (mean and range chart)
Sample is subgroup averages with subgroup sizes. Subgroup size is greater than 8	X bar S (mean and standard deviation)

In discrete data, the control chart is selected depending upon the lot size and defect/defective.

	Defects	Defectives
Constant Lot Size	C	NP
Variable Lot Size	U	P

Understanding control charts and its application in ITES industry
Example: In a multinational US bank, an LSS project was done to reduce the cycle time of the international wire transfer process from 4.76 days to one day.

Cross-functional teams across the globe were involved in this project. In the control phase of DMAIC projects, control charts help to keep a watch on the improved metric (Project Y/goal) and significant Xs which are impacting Project Y.

Control charts recommended as part of the control phase were:
1. Cycle time of international wire transfers (continuous data)
2. Processing time of each operator on different wires (continuous data)
3. Number of people absent on any given day (discrete data).

Chart 1: Cycle time of international wire transfers (continuous data).
Continuous data and subgroup size is 1 - IMR chart.

These charts can also be used to compare the before and after state of the project metrics.

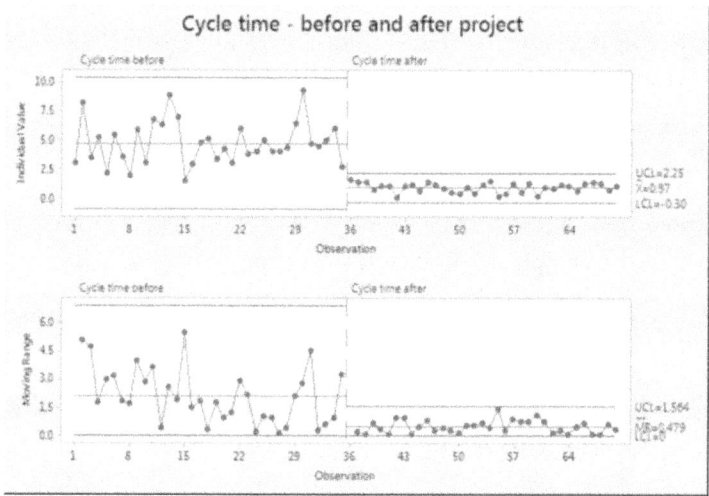

Interpretation:
The chart on the top left is cycle time before improvements and the chart on the top right is cycle time after the improvements. The chart below includes individual moving range also.

The aim of any Six Sigma project could be twofold: one is to reduce variation and two is to shift mean.

An individual chart represents the cycle time of wire transfers that indicates the central value (mean) of the data set, and the moving range represents the spread of the data (variation).

Movement of mean is quite evident, which 4.76 days to 0.97 days was. Spread of the data is also reduced from moving range of approximately 2 to 0.479

Chart 2: Processing time of each operator on different wires

X bar R control chart is called Mean and Range Chart.

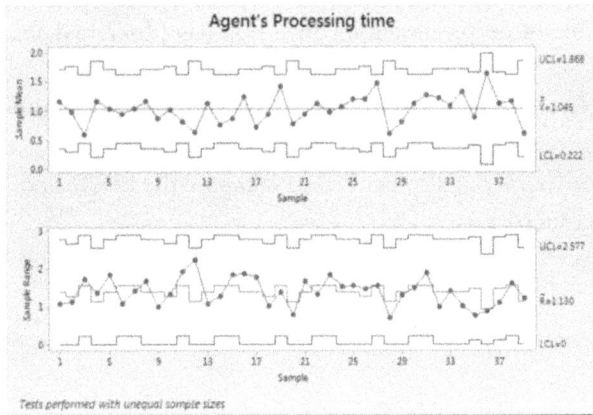

Interpretation

In this case, each operator (individual subgroup) was processing a different number of wires hourly, so the subgroup size will differ from one subgroup to another subgroup, hence the control limits are displayed in a zig-zag pattern.

The processing time of the agents is within control limits and the range is also within control.

Chart 3: Number of people absent on any given day (U chart)

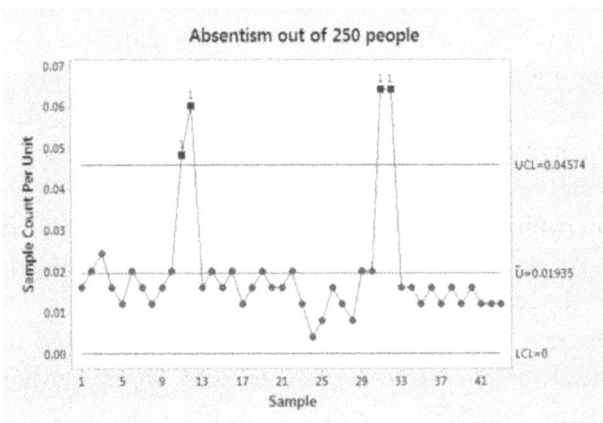

Interpretation

This graph represents the number of people absent on any given day; it shows 4 points outside the control limits. On further investigation, it was evident that there were two major festivals during that time. In order to handle the festive season properly, corrective action is recommended to be implemented going forward.

So, control charts not only help you keep a bird's eye view on the process health but can also help you improve it further.

There are various tools which can help create a control chart. However the most common tool used is Minitab.

Below is a tutorial to help you create a control chart in Minitab
IMR chart

Step 1:
Minitab Path: Stat>> Control Charts>> Variables chart for individuals>> I-MR.

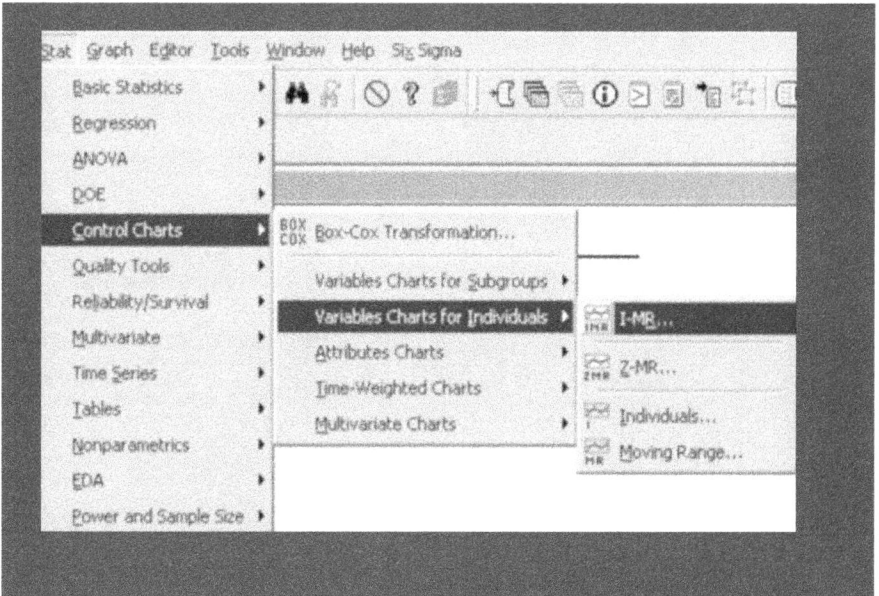

Step 2: Enter data (cycle time) in the Variable column.

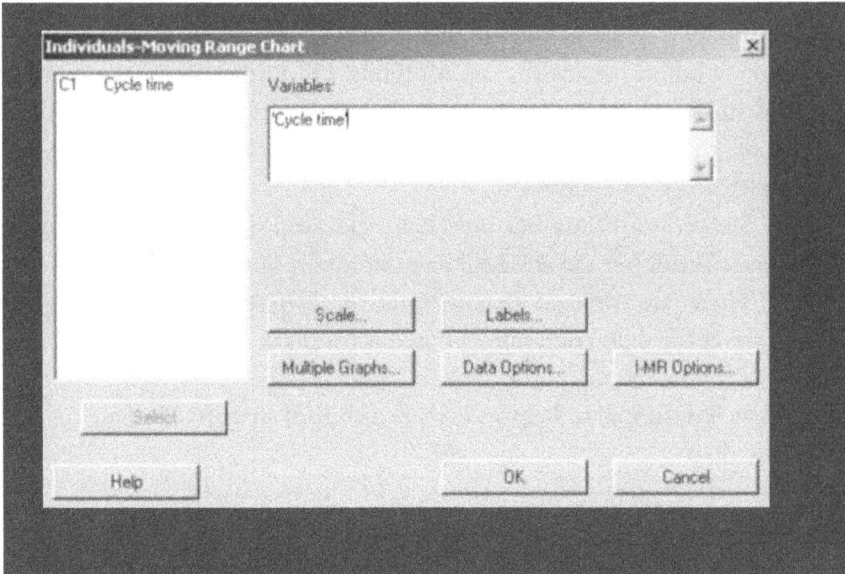

Step 3: Click Ok to get IMR chart.

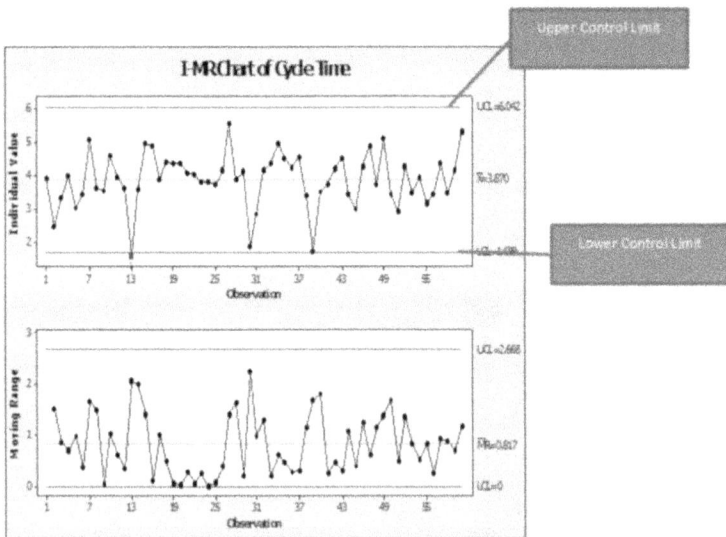

The individual chart takes care of centring and the Moving Range takes care of the spread of the data.

Use of Stages in Control Charts

There are other interpretations that can be drawn with the help of control charts; for example, before project status and after project status can be represented on the same graph, showing improvement in the metrics.

Arrange data in Minitab like shown below and follow the steps given below:

Step 1: Select Stat>>Control chart>>Variable chart for individual>> IMR Before and after project data should be stacked in one column as shown in Minitab output in column C1. In C2, add Status which will have headers like 'before project cycle time' and 'after project cycle time'.

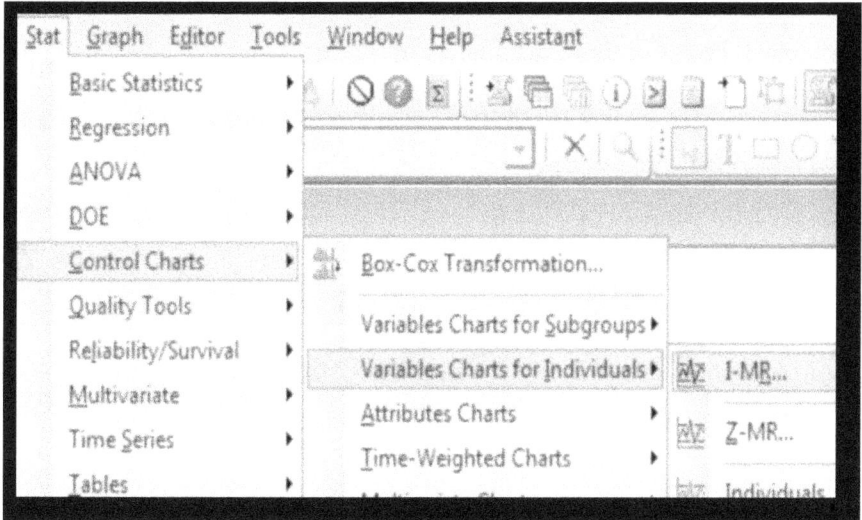

Step 2: Select Cycle Time in Variables and then go to IMR options, Go to Stages tab and select Status in that column.

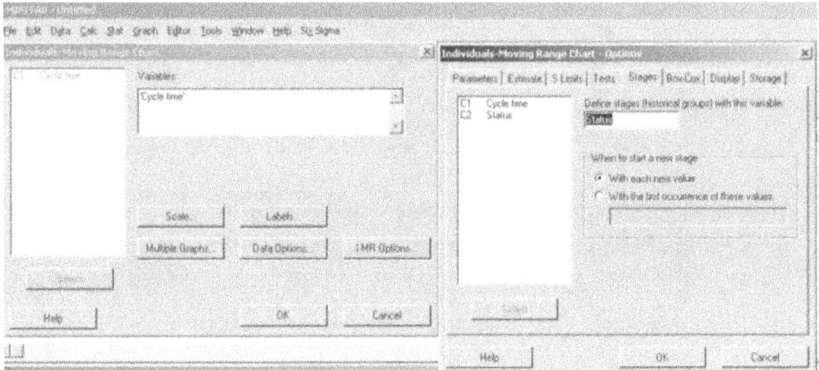

Step 3: Press OK to see the result.

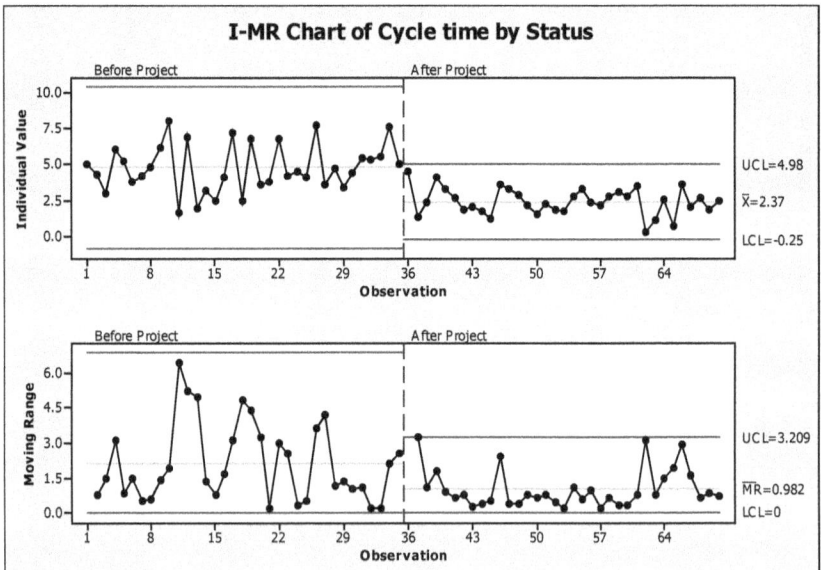

Takeaways from the graph:

1. The individual chart shows that before, the project cycle time of transactions was five minutes and after the project, it is 2.37 minutes. There is a reduction in the cycle time per transaction.

2. Moving range chart shows that the variation of the data has reduced after the project.
3. There are no special causes as well in the process.

X Bar R Chart

An X bar chart is created when the subgroup size per subgroup is between 2 ~8.

Subgroup size: Consider each agent as one subgroup, and consider the number of cases picked for each agent is 5 per day; then the subgroup size becomes 5. There is a possibility that each subgroup could have a varying subgroup size. Let us understand how we create an X bar R chart for both the instances.

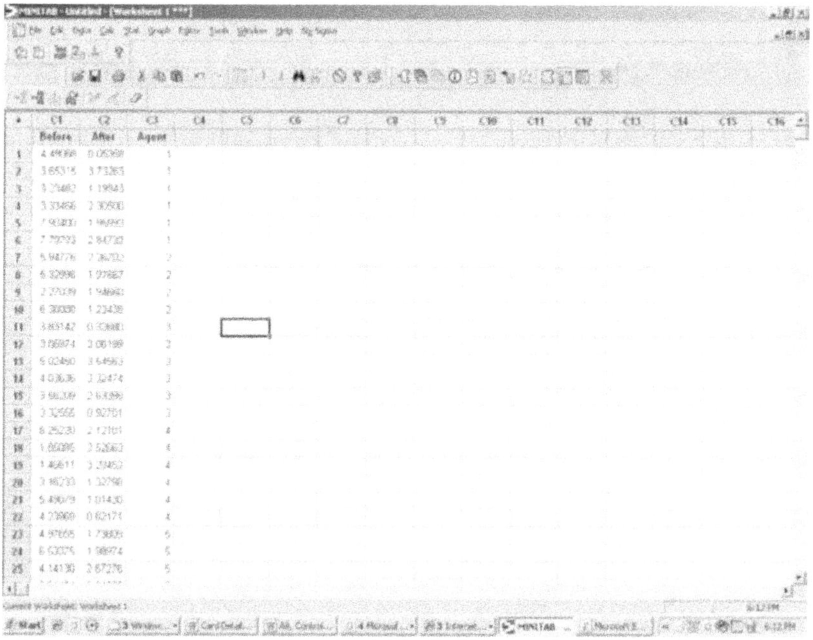

Consider that the data given is for before the Lean Six Sigma project cycle time of transactions and after the improvements are implemented; column C3 contains information on the agent who processed these transactions.

Step 1. Go to stat>>control charts>>variable charts for subgroups>> X bar R.

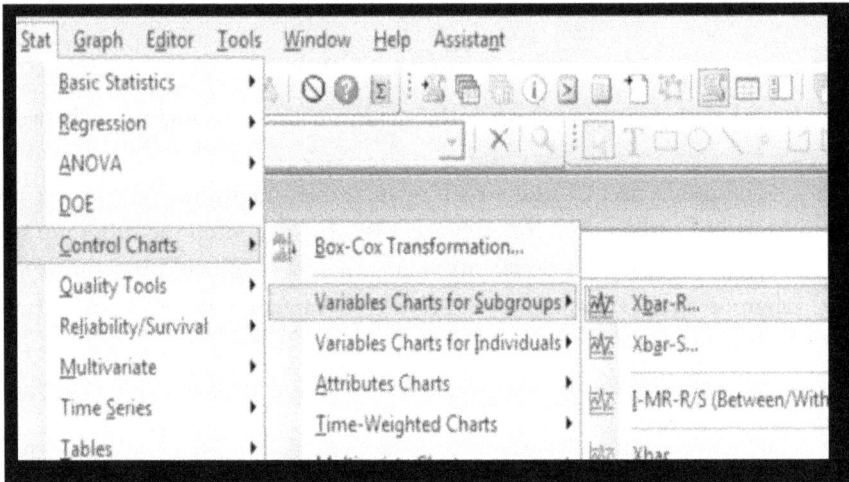

Step 2: Select Before (cycle time) and Agent in subgroup size, as sample size per agent is varying in this case, otherwise mention 5 in the sub group size if 5 transactions each were picked for each associate.

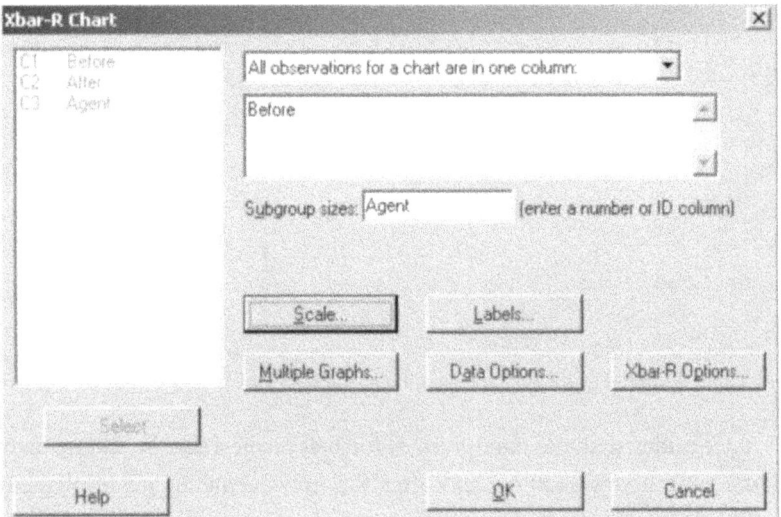

Step 3: Click OK

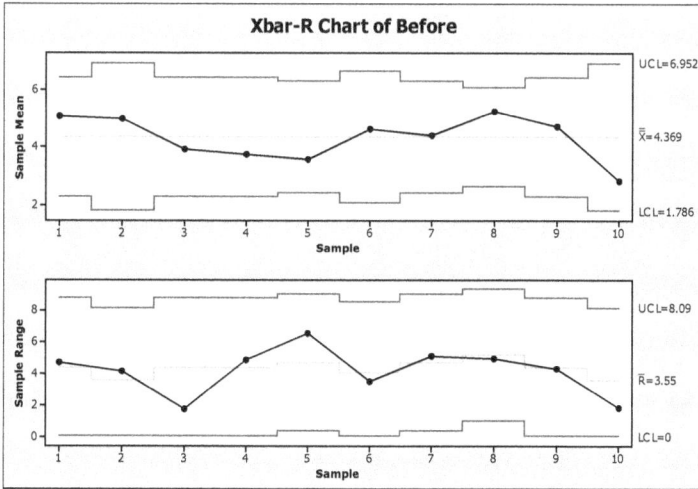

Xbar-R Chart of Before

Takeaway: Control chart X bar and R is generated and if you look at the control limits, they are varying because the subgroup size per subgroup (Agents) is varying.

X bar R with constant subgroup size for all subgroups: Look at the control chart below; if subgroup size of 5 is entered in the subgroup size cell in Minitab.

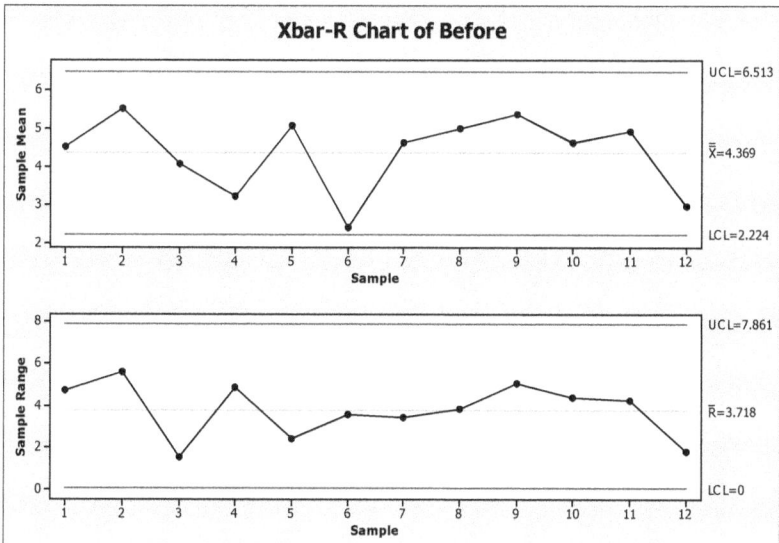

Xbar-R Chart of Before

The control limits are in a straight line.

Takeaway: In the above control chart, the X bar chart represents the variation in the central value, and R chart represents the spread of the data points.

Control Chart as Run Chart:
Interpretations which can be drawn from a run chart can also be depicted on a control chart. Run chart identifies special causes in a data set by identifying clusters, oscillations, trends etc. The same can be interpreted through control chart. Control charts provide information on special causes over and above the run chart.

Go to Options in any of the control charts. The following could be seen under header 'tests'. Select 'Perform all tests for special causes'.

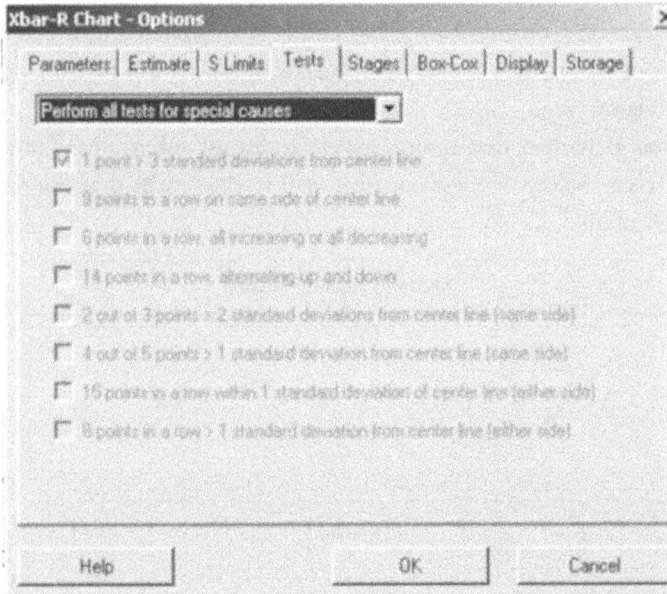

Comparisons: Tests for special causes like:
1. 9 points in a row on the same side of the centre line correspond to clustering in a run chart

2. 6 points in a row, all increasing or all decreasing, correspond to trends in a run chart

3. 14 points in a row, alternating up and down, correspond to oscillations in a run chart

There are eight tests done for special causes in continuous data control charts and four tests done for discrete data control charts.

Discrete Data - P Chart

Fixed Lot Size: Consider a situation where a client said they will do quality check for 30 processed transactions, not concerned about the transaction processed by the team.

Variable Lot Size: The customer will do a quality check on 3% of the transactions processed by the team on a daily basis. Now, when the team processes 1000 transactions, the sample size would be 30, and when the team processes 1100 transactions, the sample size will be 33; hence the lot size is varying.

For a P chart, the lot size is variable and the customer is monitoring the process on Defectives.

Consider the below-mentioned data for the chart:

Defectives	Sample Lot
12	223
11	213
12	232
14	231
12	211
16	221
12	220
10	229
9	231
12	212
11	211
10	210
17	209
12	219
12	217

8	216
9	214
9	212
9	214
10	224
11	212
11	225
13	216
9	215
12	211
14	217
12	214
12	215
18	216

Step 1: Stat>Control Chart> Attribute charts> P Chart.

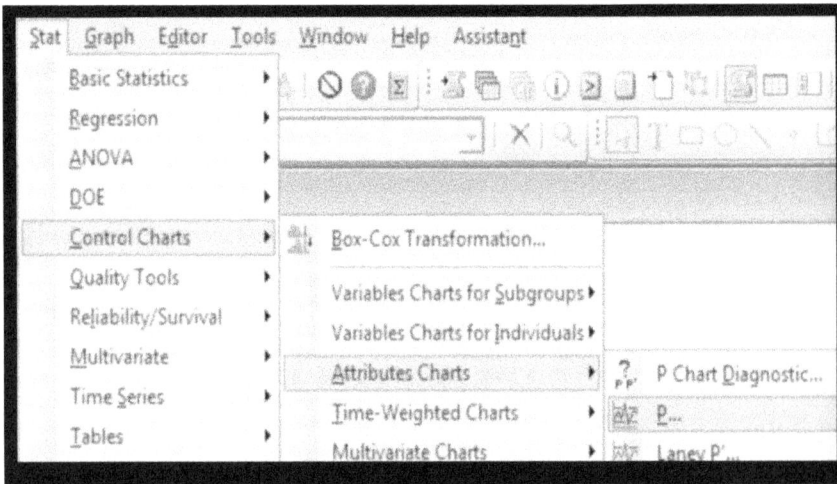

Step 2: In Variables, enter Defectives and in subgroup size, enter Sample lot.

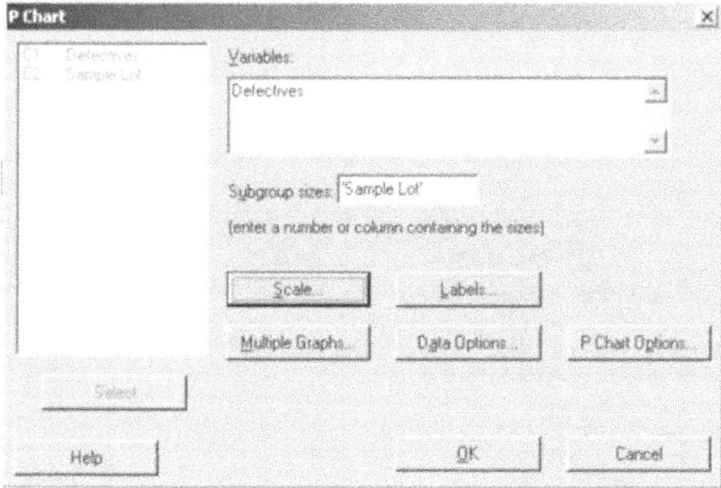

Step 3: Click ok to get the control chart.

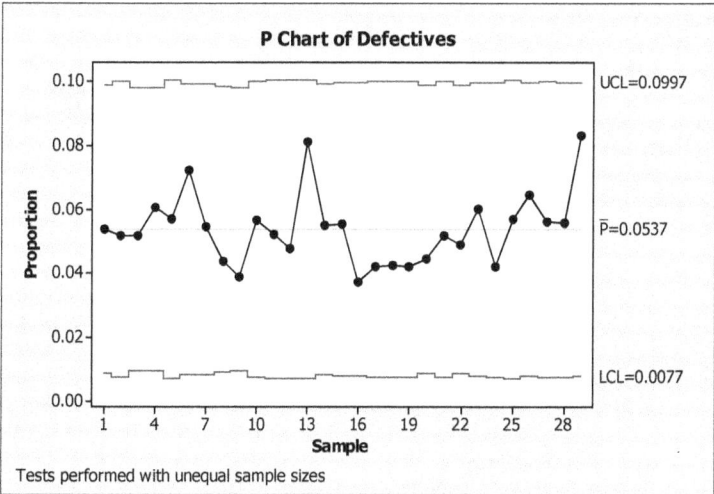

Control limits are varying because of the varying sample lot.

Control charts are a statistical tool which can help predict the special causes in business processes. They can be considered as guards for a statistical controlled process.

Refer to the case study and perform the above steps.

Create a control plan to sustain the improved process. Control plan on P1 solutions is shown below; the rest could be created as explained in the table below:

What is to be implemented	Where it is to be implemented	Who will implement	By When	How it is to be implemented	Frequency of Check	Checked by
Equal work distribution	On the floor	Team Supervisor	April 20, 2016	Work flow is to be created with the help of the IT team	Weekly	Team Manager
Create process documents for all processes	In the defined template of ISO documents and saved on a shared drive	Team SMEs	April 22, 2016	SMEs will create the document and will get it validated by customers	Fortnightly	Team Supervisor
Enhance training plan for new joiners	In the training documents on a shared drive	Training Manager	April 26, 2016	Take clues from the error sheet and enhance the training document covering the most inaccurate scenarios	Monthly	Team Manager
Train agents on all scenarios	Training room Adison	Training Manager	May 3, 2016	Train all agents on most rarely-occurring scenarios	Once, post training	Team Manager

Show improvements and sustained states through a control chart.

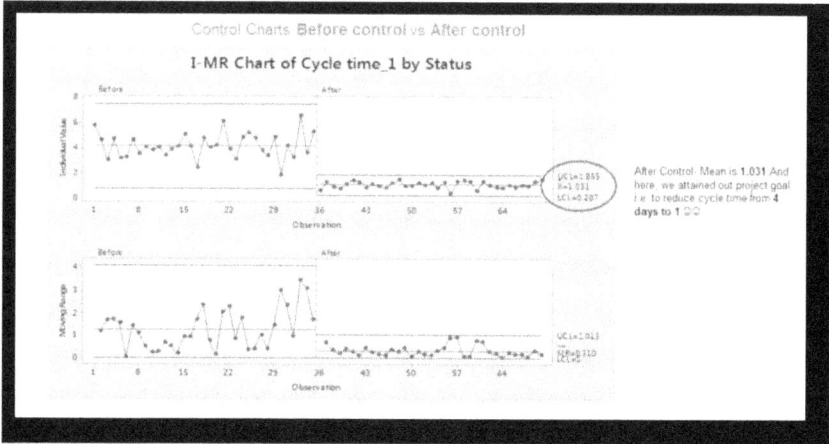

Questions for the 'control phase'.

Q1. What is a control plan? Explain its significance.

Q2. What is a control chart? Explain its significance.

Q3. Give the name of the control chart used in the scenarios below:

- Data is continuous and has a subgroup size of 3.
- Data is continuous and has a subgroup size of 1.
- Data is discrete and process is measured on defectives and the subgroup size is variable.
- Data is discrete and process is measured on defects and the subgroup size is variable.

LSS DNA building in an organisation is an integral part of the work that needs to be done as an ongoing initiative. Every Lean Six Sigma project that gets certified has to be evaluated across a minimum of three levels.

The 5-Stage DMAIC project should be evaluated at Define Stage, Analyse Stage and Closure.

A mentor should be actively involved in project reviews right from the predefine stage, asking focused questions on the team construct. Some typical, useful questions to ensure team success are:

➢ Who are the assigned Champion and Sponsor for the team?

➢ What training have the team members and the Black Belt had?

➢ Have all team members been trained?

➢ How much time does the Champion spend with your team?

➢ How often does the team meet?

➢ What is the percentage of attendance at meetings?

➢ How much time do members spend outside of meetings working on the project?

➢ Are there barriers for collaboration within the team? If so, what plans are there to address them?

➢ When did the project start? When is the planned completion date? Is the project on schedule?

➢ How is the team tracking and documenting its accomplishments?

➢ What other resources does the team need to assure success?

Define

Define the customer, their CTQs, the team charter and the business process.

Some of the critical must dos for this phase are:

➢ Customers identified and segmented as appropriate. Data to verify customers' needs and requirements, collected and plotted.

➢ Written team charter that includes rationale for project, preliminary problem statement, scope, goals, milestones, and roles and responsibilities.

➢ Completed and validated high level 'as is' process map which identifies customer, output, five to seven process blocks of activities, inputs and suppliers.

Some tools which can help in this phase are:

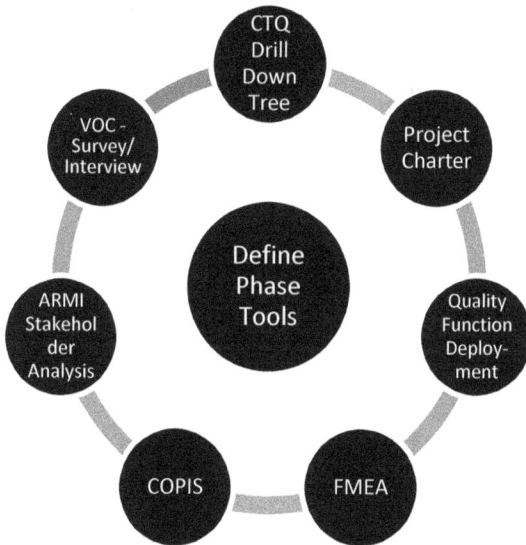

Some of the Dos and Don'ts for this phase are:

Do	Don't
The metric should be selected on the smallest unit of the process, because if the smallest unit is set right, the entire process is bound to be right. Work on direct metric not on derived metric.	Avoid dollar value as a metric, like reducing the day's sales outstanding (DSO) $30 K per day to $25 K per day. Use business impact to highlight dollar values and impact. Always choose metrics like improving hit rates of calls from 25% to 45%, hence reducing DSO. In this example, the business impact could be a DSO reduction of $5 K per day.
Pick up the actual cause of customers' problems as the project metric. Customers will always give you a practical problem; convert it to a statistical statement. E.g.: Practical problem: I am not happy with the process quality. Statistical problem: To reduce the number of defects from 20% to 5% by April 2012.	Do not take project metrics for which you cannot collect accurate or complete data. Metrics that are complex and difficult need to be explained to others. Metrics that complicate operations and create excessive overhead. Metrics that cause employees to act not in the best interests of the business but just to 'meet their numbers'.
Business case must have 'what for and why' this project is required, apart from the background of the process.	Not more than one problem statement for one project.
Slide on business impact calculation and replication projects.	
Customer signs off emails on business impact approach and charter.	

Analyse Phase

As you mentor the project successfully through the first Define stage, you now move to the Analyse phase. This phase review primarily consists of two phases of DMAIC - Measure and Analyse.

In the **Measure phase** data, the objective is to identify potential Xs, gage the measurement system and thereafter, data collection.

The deliverable of this phase is to study the business metric over time and validate the measurement system:

➤ Identify the measurable Customer CTQ.

➤ Define and confirm specifications for the Y.

➤ Ensure measurement system is adequate to measure Y.

➤ Sampling, data collection plan and measurement system analysis.

➤ Identify the potential root causes and conduct MSA (Measurement System Analysis) on the same.

Some of the tools that can be used are:

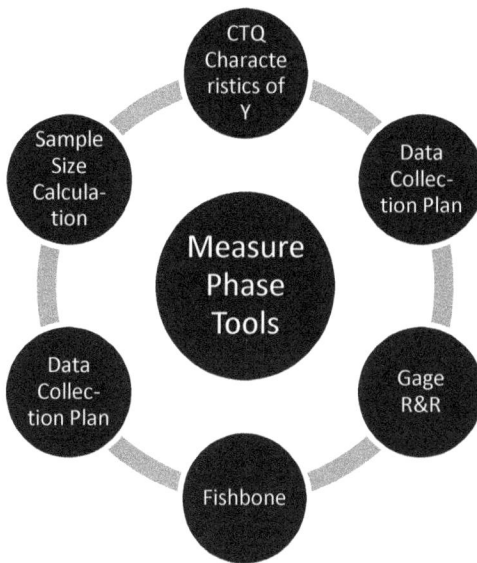

Some of the Dos and Don'ts of this phase are:

Do	Don't
Operational definition must have the mathematical formula if required.	Don't collect data on Y and potential Xs differently. Create a robust data collection plan which takes care of the entire data need in one go.
Before creating a data collection plan, identify unit, defects, opportunities and specification limits for Project Y.	Don't proceed in the project without checking the measurement system (Gage R&R).

| Identify potential Xs for project Y. It is also very important to collect data on Xs along with Y in one go. | Don't work on attribute gage with less than 20 samples. |
| There must be an action plan to correct the gage issues. The second time around, gage must pass to proceed further; otherwise repeat the entire process till the time gage passes. | For repeatability, there should not be less than a week's time in between two trials of the same operator. |

In **the third phase** (Analyse) of DMAIC, the major deliverables are: Identify current performance, future goal and root cause affecting CTQ.

➤ A detailed 'AS-IS' process map, analysed using value/non-value added steps and cycle time/wait time tools the 'vital few' factors.
➤ A rationale for why the above approach was chosen.
➤ A refined problem statement reflecting the increased understanding of the problem gained from the analysis.
➤ Estimated dollar value benefits.
  Some of the useful tools that can be referred to in this phase are:

The most important tool in the analyse phase is Hypothesis testing. Listed below are some useful tips.

Hypothesis test selection: Hypothesis tests should be selected based on the following graph:

	Y Continuous - Normal	Y Continuous – Non-Normal	Y Discrete
X continuous	Simple linear regression		Logistic regression
X discrete 1 variable 2 variables 2 or more than 2 variable Checking Variation	1T 2T One Way Annova	1 Sample Wilcoxon Mann Whitney Mood's Median	1P 2P Chi Square
	Test for Equal Variance		

P-Value:

Alpha is the maximum acceptable probability of being wrong if the alternate hypothesis is selected.

The **P-value** is the **probability that you will be wrong if you select the alternate hypothesis.**

Unless there is an exception based on engineering judgment, we will set an acceptance level of **P** at alpha = 0.05.

Thus, any P-value less than 0.05 means we reject the null hypothesis.

Some Dos and Don'ts of this phase are:

Do	Don't
All the Xs should have the same number of data points for hypothesis tests.	Do not leave any potential X (non-significant X), thinking it is not important. Do either of the two data validations or NGT before taking a decision on all the Xs.
Work on data door Xs through hypothesis and use tools like nominal group techniques for Process door Xs	

Closure Phase

There are two stages of the DMAIC methodology which are part of the Closure phase – Improve and Control.

Improve: After identifying the significant Xs, now identify the root causes for the significant Xs, then do the pilot and implement the solution for the entire team.

Some of the key deliverables are:

➢ Generate, select, design and implement practical improvements.
➢ Identify a vital few Xs and develop practical solutions for the same.
➢ Conduct pilot of improvements and measure against specifications.
➢ Specify tolerance limits on the vital few Xs with cost/benefit proposal presented.
➢ Develop the change management plan and translate solution (vision) to behaviours.
➢ Mobilise commitment and conduct systems and structures modifications (e.g., staffing, training, measurement/reward systems, structure, IT systems, communications).
➢ Build communication plan and execute change.

Some of the relevant tools for this phase are:

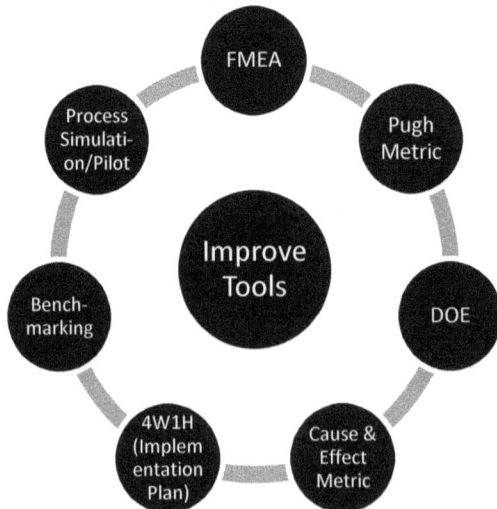

Some Dos and Don'ts of this phase are:

Do	Don't
Identify solutions for all the significant Xs identified for process door and data door Xs.	Don't implement any big change or solution before piloting the solution.
Do use 5 Why analysis as a must in this phase to identify root causes and solutions.	Don't implement any big change or solution before FMEA.

Control Phase

The control phase is the most critical phase of the improvement initiative. Some of the important deliverables of this phase are:

➢ Institutionalise the improvement and implement ongoing monitoring.
➢ Transfer improvements through measurement system application.
➢ Develop a control plan with FMEA and a communication plan.
➢ Measure process capability post improvements and highlight improvements (pre & post).
➢ Build review mechanism and document procedures.
➢ Conduct customer VOC to measure the impact.
➢ Business impact sign off and realisation.
➢ Sustain change through control plan.

Some of the relevant tools that can be used for this phase are:

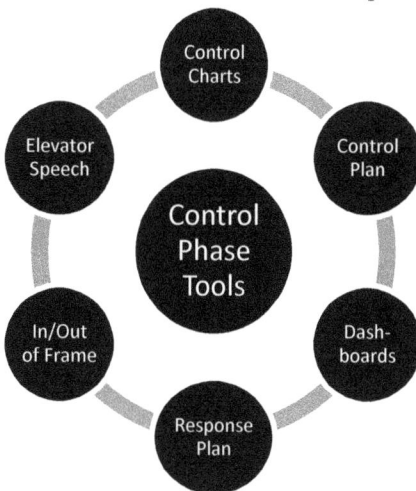

Useful Tips:

There are different types of control charts available. To identify a control chart for different data types we can look at the description below.

It is recommended that for continuous data you can use three control charts and for discrete, there are four.

S. No.	Continuous Data	Discrete Data
1	IMR	C
2	X Bar R	U
3	X Bar S	P
4		Np

In continuous data, the control chart is selected depending on the subgroup size.

Description	Control Chart
Sample is individual measurement. Subgroup size is one	IMR (Individual Moving Range)
Sample is subgroup averages with subgroup sizes Subgroup size is 2~8	X bar R (Mean and Range Chart)
Sample is subgroup averages with subgroup sizes Subgroup size is greater than 8	X bar S (Mean and Standard deviation)

In discrete data, the control chart is selected depending upon the lot size and Defect/Defective.

	Defects	Defectives
Constant Lot Size	C	NP
Variable Lot Size	U	P

Some of the Dos and Don'ts for this phase are:

Do	Don't
Check for Control plan on both Project Y and Significant Xs.	Don't miss plotting the control charts on Significant Xs wherever possible - like IMR chart for break time and P chart for absenteeism - if they are Significant Xs proved in the analyse phase.
Do track the control plan on a periodic basis as frequency of check defined in the control plan.	Don't forget to create a control chart for project Y also, as there could be another factor that might start impacting Project Y other than significant Xs already identified. So, tracking output is also important.

If a DMAIC project is mentored and evaluated at each phase, the right questions are asked, and relevant tools are used, then a high-quality output within a stipulated time can be expected. This chapter will help Black Belts and Master Black Belts enhance mentoring effectiveness of LSS projects, as it can be referred as a ready reckoner or a pocket guide.

Mohit Sharma is a certified Master Black Belt from Genpact and a certified Black Belt and Green Belt from ASQ and Motorola University.

He is a privileged member of the ASQ's (American Society of Quality) Technical Board for reviewing and approving LSS articles and manuscripts. His White Papers are published in external publications and are highly appreciated by readers.

He has bagged many prestigious awards for his Six Sigma work and projects which include:

- Commendation Award by the Indian Statistical Institute, Bangalore 2017,
- Silver Award at QCI – DL Shah Quality Awards at National level 2016,
- SSON (Shared Services & Outsourcing Network)
- The Excellence Award from ASQ quality.

Mohit Sharma has a knack of simplifying jargon by effectively writing his Six Sigma experiences and perceptions and sharing his deep knowledge of the subject with his readers.

He is an Electronics and Communication Engineer and an MBA in Marketing by qualification.